D1539052

YOU WORK TOMORROW

CLASS : CULTURE

SERIES EDITORS
Amy Schrager Lang, Syracuse University, and
Bill V. Mullen, Purdue University

EDITORIAL BOARD
Nicholas Bromell, University of Massachusetts
Nan Enstad, University of Wisconsin
Amy Gluckman, *Dollars and Sense*
Leslie Harris, Emory University
Cora Kaplan, University of Southampton
Louis Mendoza, University of Minnesota
Jonathan Prude, Emory University
Steven Ross, University of Southern California
Cecelia Tichi, Vanderbilt University
Lisa Yun, Binghamton University
Alan Wald, University of Michigan
Janet Zandy, Rochester Institute of Technology

TITLES IN THE SERIES:

You Work Tomorrow: An Anthology of American Labor Poetry, 1929–41
Edited by John Marsh

The Syntax of Class: Writing Inequality in Nineteenth-Century America
Amy Schrager Lang

Vanishing Moments: Class and American Culture
Eric Schocket

Let Me Live
Angelo Herndon

Workin' on the Chain Gang: Shaking Off the Dead Hand of History
Walter Mosley

Commerce in Color: Race, Consumer Culture, and American Literature, 1893–1933
James C. Davis

You Work Tomorrow

AN ANTHOLOGY OF AMERICAN
LABOR POETRY, 1929–41

EDITED BY John Marsh

FOREWORD BY Jim Daniels

The University of Michigan Press

Ann Arbor

Copyright © by the University of Michigan 2007
All rights reserved
Published in the United States of America by
The University of Michigan Press
Manufactured in the United States of America
⊗ Printed on acid-free paper

2010 2009 2008 2007   4 3 2 1

No part of this publication may be reproduced, stored in a retrieval system,
or transmitted in any form or by any means, electronic, mechanical, or otherwise,
without the written permission of the publisher.

A CIP catalog record for this book is available from the British Library.

Library of Congress Cataloging-in-Publication Data

You work tomorrow: an anthology of American labor poetry, 1929–41 /
    edited by John Marsh; foreword by Jim Daniels.
        p. cm. — (Class, culture)
    Includes index.
    ISBN-13: 978-0-472-07000-8 (acid-free paper)
    ISBN-10: 0-472-07000-2 (acid-free paper)
    ISBN-13: 978-0-472-05000-0 (pbk.: acid-free paper)
    ISBN-10: 0-472-05000-1 (pbk.: acid-free paper)
    1. Working class writings, American.   2. American poetry—20th
century.   3. Working class—Poetry.   4. Labor—Poetry.   5. Labor
movement—Poetry.   I. Marsh, John, 1975–

PS591.W65Y68   2007
811',52083553—dc22   2007031016

For our silenced people, century after century their beings consumed in the hard, everyday essential work of maintaining human life. Their art, which still they made—as their other contributions—anonymous; refused respect, recognition; lost.

—Tillie Olsen, *Silences*

It is part of the insult offered to intelligence by a class-society that this history of ordinary thought is ever found surprising.

—Raymond Williams, *The Country and the City*

Foreword

JIM DANIELS

You have in front of you both an important historical document and an important contribution to our literature—not only labor literature, but the larger world of literature that has so often dismissed or ignored poetry from workers. Writing poetry is at least in part an act of preservation—of saving memory, emotion—and the poems in *You Work Tomorrow: An Anthology of American Labor Poetry, 1929–41* do just that. They preserve a time in American labor history that was volatile, political, and passionate. But writing poetry is also an act of *self*-preservation, a way for people to express themselves as a way of surviving the difficulties of their daily lives—their daily *working* lives—and these poems do that too.

These poems originally were published in union publications, and they haven't seen the light of day in many, many years. What has been forgotten and ignored has now been reclaimed by John Marsh so that these workers' voices can again be heard and listened to. They have been preserved *once again*. It is a cause for celebration and for a sober examination of the place of work in our cultural heritage then and now. Marsh's thorough, informative introduction helps to contextualize these poems so that we can appreciate and understand who wrote them and why. The poems, together with Marsh's introduction and comprehensive notes, reveal the range of individual voices that spoke up and were heard. The impressive variety of voices contradicts any stereotype or generalization that one might attempt to impose on the workers of this era.

The poems are often surprisingly humorous, satirical. The poets riff on nursery rhymes, popular songs, movies, prayers—even recipes. They know what's up and are leery of any authority that claims to know what's best for them. They recognize the enormous disparity between the rich and the poor. While they didn't have the power that the companies and the government had, they at least had the power to tell the truth about the state of labor in their individual occupations, and in the country as a whole. One theme that runs through many of these poems is the simple notion of solidarity—that we're in this together, and we need to stick together to have any hope of changing things, of improving salaries and working conditions.

If some of these poets sound like cheerleaders, they are not the traditional cheerleaders from the sidelines; they are voices from the front lines of labor and the union movement. Veterans of the picket lines, and the assembly lines, and the unemployment lines, they are smart, articulate, and passionate cheerleaders who often express their feelings with a hint of desperation, for there is more than the outcome of a game at stake—it's their lives, their livelihoods, that are on the line. The poets speak with the passion and authority of insiders, writing knowledgeably about the work they do and how it makes them feel. The poems exist not simply as historic relics, but as fresh reminders for today's readers of the importance of recording and remembering injustice, and the place of individual voices within the larger community of workers—and how, when many of those voices are brought together, as they are here, they create a force that cannot be overlooked, cannot be left out of our literary and cultural history.

Despite the hardships and struggles expressed in many of these poems, this collection represents a celebration of the spirit of the American labor movement, for the poems here move from coast to coast, from occupation to occupation, from union to union. When I think about the American spirit, I think not of flag-waving patriotism and the self-righteous belief in the superiority of the "American way." Instead, I think of voices like those in these poems. Voices that have earned their right to speak through hard work and experience. Voices stubbornly independent and full of personal self-sacrifice and compassion for others. Reading these poems, I can't help but feel a little wistful. They take us back to a slice of American history in which the possibilities for change existed, a time in which workers could decry their working conditions with the sincere hope that somebody might be listening. No one would want to return to those days of hardship and struggle, but I do long for the independent spirit of those voices, the gritty wit, the passion and compassion of voices speaking up in support of a cause.

Acknowledgments

It feels inappropriate to acknowledge anyone but the poets and workers who wrote the poems and organized the unions that made this anthology possible in the first place; even so, it feels equally inappropriate not to acknowledge the many people who have helped to bring their work the new readers it deserves. Debra Hawhee encouraged the project from the first moment I offhandedly mentioned it. James Barrett taught me about labor history and clued me in to the cultural work of the United Electrical Workers before the project even began in earnest. David Roediger provided early advice regarding presses. William Maxwell helped me put together a book proposal. Judith Siporin, Miriam Tane's daughter, provided invaluable biographical information and made me realize that many people already remembered and prized this poetry. Nicholas Coles read a late draft of the manuscript and had valuable advice to give. Jim Daniels wrote a foreword that reminded me why I started work on this anthology at all. Several outside readers offered careful reviews of the manuscript and improved it throughout. Cary Nelson taught me about the variety of modern American poetry and recognized the significance of this poetry from the start. Michael Honey helped me connect John Henry of the Southern Tenant Farmers Union to John Handcox. Finally, my deepest thanks go to Amy Lang, Bill Mullen, Anna Szymanski, and LeAnn Fields—especially LeAnn—for their work on the Class: Culture Series at the University of Michigan Press and for seeing this book into print.

I would like to thank all those individuals that granted permission to reprint poems in this anthology, including Camellia Cook, David Giovannitti, Richard Rorty, and Judith Siporin. I have done my best to contact copyright owners to obtain permission, but, as with my attempts to learn biographical details about the poets in this collection, that has not always been possible. Many poets wrote anonymously or under pseudonyms, and those who did not have proven difficult to locate. Needless to say, I welcome further inquiries.

Contents

Introduction:
The Turbulent Poetics of 1930s Labor Poetry / 1

PART I: AMERICAN FEDERATION OF LABOR

American Federation of Musicians / 33
Gertrude Munter / 34
The Wizard of Robot
Mr. Modestus / 36
Men are asking for work
Adventure

American Federation of Teachers / 40
Nell Owen / 40
Just Another Day
E. H. H. Holman / 43
Amos 'n Andy

Associated Actors and Artistes of America / 44
Peter Donald, Jr. / 45
Revenge without Music
Ann Winthrop / 46
Reverie
Lee Willoughby / 46
Don't Bite the Hand
Frances Scanlin / 47
Questionnaire for Actors

Brotherhood of Maintenance of Way Employes / 49
Thomas R. Lynch / 49
  Begging for Bread
Edna Jacques / 51
  Working Mother's Prayer
Gequel / 52
  Company Unionism

Brotherhood of Sleeping Car Porters / 54
Bennie Smith / 55
  Stick, Boys!
Aseneth Cargill / 56
  Discernment
Anonymous / 56
  Brighter Ash

International Fur and Leather Workers Union / 57
Anonymous / 57
  The Label Tells a Story

**Hotel and Restaurant Employees
and Bartenders International Union** / 59
Martin A. Dillman / 59
  Waitresses' Union No. 249
James M. Bishop / 61
  A Square Deal or a "Quare" Deal
Anonymous / 62
  Supreme Court

International Association of Machinists / 63
Rose Elizabeth Smith / 64
  The Ninety and Nine
Anonymous / 65
  Surplus Value
Thomas H. West / 65
  While Playing Santa Claus

**United Brotherhood of Carpenters
and Joiners of America** / 67
Bud McKillups / 68
  Labor

C. Lender / 69
From an Old-Timer

United Textile Workers of America / 71
Modestus / 72
Why, oh why?
Fibres
"Trust in the Profit System!"

PART II: UNAFFILIATED UNIONS

Industrial Workers of the World / 81
Lola Nolan / 83
Grin, Clown, Grin
Covington Ami / 84
Confessions
Anonymous / 85
The Skid Road
William Patton / 86
Nix
T-Bone Slim / 87
Turning the Corner
    (The Romantic Quest of Lost Love)
Ralph Chaplin / 88
Harlan
William E. Patton / 89
The Sin of Hoarding
310 Bulletin / 91
Heat Portraits
Jack Kenney / 92
The Migratory I.W.W.
Harold Allinger / 93
Hell
Left Rudder / 94
The Shape Up
Robert Whitaker / 95
Madrid
John G. Hirschfeldt / 96
The Line-Up

Covington Hall / 97
   Surpluses, O the Surpluses!
   The Curious Christians
Anonymous / 99
   To a Nine-Inch Gun
Albert Brocken / 100
   To the Spinachers

Sailors Union of the Pacific / 102
R. F. Steltemeier / 102
   The Company Union
Anonymous / 103
   The Live One
Anonymous / 104
   A Brother's Complaint

Southern Tenant Farmers' Union / 108
Anonymous / 110
   Share-Cropper's Choice
Anonymous / 110
   The Sharecropper
Covington Hall / 111
   Good Ol' Pete
John Henry (John Handcox) / 112
   The Planter and the Sharecropper
   Landlord, What in the Heaven is the Matter with You?
   The Union Song

PART III: CONGRESS OF INDUSTRIAL ORGANIZATIONS

International Ladies Garment Workers Union / 119
Nahum Yood / 121
   In a Garment Factory
Arturo Giovannitti / 122
   The Final Installment
Martha Stevenson / 124
   Freedom
Max Press / 125
   The I.L.G.W.U.

Mr. Modestus   /   126
  We talk of progress
  It's a stick-up!
Jessie Carter   /   130
  On Hearing a Negro Spiritual
Arturo Giovannitti   /   131
  All-Fighters Day
Syde Waller   /   134
  What Do You Build?
Hilda W. Smith   /   135
  Labor Stage
Max Press   /   136
  To Whom It May Concern . . .
Miriam Tane   /   137
  Spring
  Factory Windows
  Stitching Machine
  Dignity
  Evacuations
  Headline Fugitive
  Day in Technicolor
  Night Fog
  Blue-Eyed Pigeon
  Parent Prayer
  Morning
  Cafeteria

International Sailors Union
(National Maritime Union of America)   /   151
Left Rudder   /   151
  Eight Bells
J. Freeman   /   153
  For Seven Years I've Roamed the Seas
Forty Fathoms   /   154
  Shipowners' "Days" . . .
Willie Sue Blagden   /   155
  To the Seamen of the International Brigade

Anonymous / 156
  My Picket Card
Forty Fathoms / 158
  Dreams 1914–1918
  Blind Justice
  The Negro Seaman Speaks
  The Slogan

United Auto Workers / 165
John Paine / 167
  King Henry the V-8th
Canadian Ford Worker / 168
  A Ford Slave
Anonymous / 169
  Letting the Cat out of the Bag
Tekla Roy / 170
  Beefsteak Blues
Clayton Fountain / 171
  To Alfred P. Sloan
George F. Young / 172
  What We Want
Murray Roth / 172
  A Stoolie's Lament
Elizabeth England / 173
  The House That Jack Built
George A. Medalis / 176
  Thursday Afternoons
Francis Reardon / 176
  As Uncle Henry Would Have Us Pray
Murray Roth / 177
  Dearborn Hospitality
Ralph H. Marlatt / 178
  I am the picket
  Detroit
  Have you ever worked on a line puttin' out
    five thousand bodies a day?
  We are the auto workers

Anonymous / 183
  The people
Tobie / 184
  Fordism
Anonymous / 184
  Ford Sunday Evening Hour
Poll / 187
  pressure
  "you work tomorrow"

**United Electrical, Radio, and
Machine Workers of America** / 192
Walter Mugford / 193
  The Five-Point Plan
  Help!
Floyd C. Bates / 195
  Lament of a Michigander
Walter Mugford / 197
  "Never Again"
Al Rimer / 199
  Real Americans
Jack McGowan / 199
  A Helper's Prayer

United Mine Workers of America / 201
Joseph Poggianni / 203
  Children of the Mine
Anonymous (From Mingo County) / 203
  Verses from West Virginia
Lou Barrelle and Andy Lucas / 205
  Pick Coal Rhythm
Billy H. Quinn / 206
  The Fatal Gilberton Mine
John Hackenbury / 208
  When Daddy Gets a Raise
Nettie M. Schoneman / 210
  The Coal-Miner's Blues

Anonymous / 211
  Union Stew
W. I. Williams / 212
  Machinery vs. Men
Anonymous / 213
  The Miner

United Packinghouse Workers of America / 214
Ivan Soelberg / 215
  The Speed King

United Rubber Workers / 217
Mary Lechner / 217
  If This Be My Native Land

United Steel Workers / 219
James Rorty / 220
  Here Goes Steel!

Index of Poems and Poets / 221

YOU WORK TOMORROW

Introduction

The Turbulent Poetics of 1930s Labor Poetry

The standard history of labor in the 1930s calls that decade simply the "tur-
bulent years," and with good cause.[1] Even before the stock market crashed on
October 24, 1929 ("Black Thursday") businesses had begun to curtail produc-
tion and lay off workers. And after the stock market crash, the economic con-
traction turned into a full-on depression. In December 1929, four million
workers were unemployed. By spring of 1933, in contrast, some fifteen million
(roughly one out of every three workers) had no job, and millions more
worked only part-time. By 1931, five thousand banks had failed, and some
nine million people lost whatever money they had managed to save. Bread-
lines and soup kitchens formed in every major city, even though local relief
funds quickly evaporated—and federal funds arrived slowly if at all. Many
people could no longer pay their rent or mortgage and so moved into
makeshift camps on the outskirts of cities—named "Hoovervilles" after the
largely ineffectual president, Herbert H. Hoover. By 1932, farmers earned just
two-thirds what they had in 1929; many had to declare bankruptcy and many
lost their farms altogether. Drought descended upon the Great Plains, while
dust storms—essentially walls of dirt—rolled across parts of Kansas, Okla-
homa, Colorado, New Mexico, and the Texas Panhandle, destroying crops
and livestock and driving over three million people off the land.[2]

In January 1937, Franklin Roosevelt surveyed the country and offered
his famously bleak portrait of "one-third of a nation ill-housed, ill-clad, and
ill-nourished."

Turbulence, though, literally means a stirred up crowd, an etymology that
might remind us that in the 1930s turbulence did not just fall on workers and
their families from on high in the form of economic depression and despair,

but that workers and their families kicked up a good deal of it themselves. Indeed, more than perhaps any other decade, we view the 1930s through an almost permanent cloud of tear gas, and the strikes, marches, and massacres of that period have become legendary.

In 1934, Congress passed the National Industrial Recovery Act, which temporarily (the Supreme Court would later overturn it) endorsed the right of workers "to organize and bargain collectively through representatives of their own choosing." The act did little to force employers to honor that right, but it nevertheless inspired some ailing American Federation of Labor unions—the United Mine Workers of America and the International Ladies Garment Workers Union especially—to launch organizing drives, to call strikes, and to win major gains for their workers. More violent, though frequently less successful, were the series of mass and general strikes in 1934 led by migrant farm laborers in California, auto parts workers in Toledo, teamsters in Minneapolis, longshoremen in San Francisco, and textile workers—some 376,000—all along the Atlantic Coast.

At the same time, workers in the new, mass-production industries—steel, automobile, rubber, radio and electrical appliances—also began to stir themselves and organize. These industrial workers, however, did not readily fit into the structure of the AFL or its affiliates, which usually organized workers by their skill or craft—carpenter, electrician, machinist—regardless of where or for whom they worked. Instead, these semiskilled workers both turned toward and made possible a new union structure, one that would remake the labor movement and the country itself in the second half of the 1930s. Motivated by workers' growing discontent and by passage of the Wagner Act in 1935— which granted workers the right to form a union after the Supreme Court ruled the earlier NRA unconstitutional—the newly formed Congress of Industrial Organizations, led by the United Mine Workers of America president John L. Lewis, set out to organize the millions of unorganized mass-production workers neglected by or disgusted with the craft-oriented American Federation of Labor.

In December 1936, autoworkers in Flint, Michigan, took control of several General Motors factories and began what would turn into a forty-four-day "sit-down" strike to win national recognition for their fledgling, somewhat disorganized, and CIO-affiliated union, the United Auto Workers. When the historically antiunion General Motors eventually capitulated and signed a contract with the striking workers, the victory reverberated across the nation. U.S. Steel president Myron Taylor believed it signaled that "complete industrial organization was inevitable," and so it more or less did. Taylor himself later signed an agreement with CIO-backed steelworkers, and in the months that followed, workers sat down or walked off their jobs in the rubber, auto, meatpacking, electrical equipment, textile, trucking, and dock work industries, among others. In 1938, 4.7 million workers would take part in a strike, and by the fall of that year, 3.7 million of them had joined or affiliated with CIO unions.

What does all this turbulence have to do with the supposedly unturbulent genre of poetry? To answer that question, we need to appreciate just how much the 1930s experienced a cultural revolt as well as a labor one. Horrified by the Great Depression and inspired by workers' responses to it, many writers, artists, critics, and culture workers—sometimes though not always aligned with the increasingly influential Communist Party of the United States of America—sought to remake the nation's literary and cultural domains. "Go Left, Young Writer!" the irascible literary Communist Mike Gold urged in 1929, and many heeded his call. In the late 1920s and early 1930s, previously unpublished worker-writers found a home for their literary ambitions in the CPUSA-backed literary journal *New Masses* (edited by Gold) and the many—also sponsored by the CPUSA—magazines and journals published by local literary organizations, the John Reed Clubs, which sprang up in most major industrial cities. But even more established writers of the 1930s turned toward producing fiction, poetry, reportage, drama, and even literary criticism that could document the exploitation and suffering of the working class and (they hoped) help make good on its revolutionary potential.[3]

While labor historians have long had to makes sense of the turbulent 1930s, the disciplines of English and literary criticism have lagged behind. Indeed, with the exception of the occasional anthology and a handful of critical works, for roughly fifty years the literary 1930s remained taboo to a discipline still influenced by the anti-Communist zeitgeist of the Cold War and by the poetic and political prejudices of the New Criticism. All that has changed in the past two decades, though, and the proletarian and Popular Front phases of 1930s culture have recently attracted the attention of literary scholars and cultural historians.[4] For the most part, however, critics have focused on those literary and cultural figures who may have sympathized with, identified with, and sought to advance the interests of workers, but who nevertheless considered themselves primarily writers, directors, performers, or other culture workers. Moreover, critical focus has tended to remain on the sphere of writers and artists affiliated with, fellow-traveling with, or reacting against the

Communist Party and its various literary organs and programs. Curiously, though, for all the recent attention paid to the culture—literary and popular, leftist and mainstream—of what one prominent scholar has called "the age of the CIO," few critics or anthologists have examined the literary and cultural products of the workers and organizers who made that age the age of the CIO in the first place—that is, the literary and cultural products of workers and labor organizers themselves.[5]

To be sure, one cannot for long maintain hard-and-fast divisions among all these literary, labor, and left figures and organizations in the 1930s. After all, many of the CIO's best organizers were Communists, the left-wing poet Edwin Rolfe briefly edited *Furniture Worker,* the newspaper of the Furniture Workers Union, and some of the poets in this collection were members of the Communist Party as well as members of their respective unions. Some may have even wished to make writing their vocation and not just their avocation. Nevertheless, and regardless perhaps of the cause, the unarguable effect has been that recent anthologists and critics have tended to neglect individuals who considered themselves workers or organizers first and poets or writers second—if at all—but who nevertheless produced, as this anthology attests, much work of literary value and interest.

Indeed, as autoworkers continued to occupy General Motors factories in Flint in January 1937, the *United Auto Worker* published some half dozen of the songs workers and their auxiliaries had composed and sung in the course of their ongoing strike. "The practice," the *United Auto Worker* noted of such songs, "was universal," and the editors of the newspaper linked this "creative activity" to the "veritable up-surge of creative activity along the lines of letter-writing, poetry, drawing, etc. among our people since the strikes began." "What work has already been done," the UAW editors concluded, "is only a slight indication of the vast creative resources possessed by the American working people."

With notable exceptions, then, and for the reasons suggested above, workers' collective creative activity in the 1930s has gone relatively undocumented. The anthology that follows, therefore, is devoted to the recovery of one of the genres—poetry—into which American working people channeled their (as the *United Auto Worker* put it) vast creative resources. Throughout the 1930s, but especially in the latter half of that decade, hundreds, easily thousands of workers—not just autoworkers but also musicians, teachers, actors, sleeping car porters, bartenders, waitresses, machinists, carpenters, textile workers, sailors, tenant farmers, garment workers, appliance manufacturers, packinghouse workers, miners—would write poems and see them printed in their AFL, CIO, and unaffiliated union newspapers. As a whole, those poems offer some of the most immediate and oftentimes moving evocations of working, living, and political conditions during the Great Depression, the efforts of workers to change those conditions, and the recalcitrance and resistance those efforts more often than not met from their employers, and, sometimes, the state. In other words, in these turbulent times, many workers responded with equally turbulent poems. Moreover, far from the way a generation of literary critics has mistakenly characterized left poetry of the 1930s—that is, as slightly embarrassing or amateurish sloganeering—the poetry workers wrote during this period is ceaselessly inventive, oftentimes unexpectedly funny, wickedly satiric, and realized in a variety of poetic forms and techniques.

Whether because of what they say or how they say it, then, these poems constitute a regrettably neglected moment in the history of modern American poetry and the history of the American labor movement. It is the aim of this collection to help restore these poems and the category of labor poetry more generally to their deserved place in our literary and social history. In addition to helping us understand the cultural and political work they may have done in their own time, it is also my hope that these poets and their poems will do cultural work *today,* not the least of which is to remind us of a collective, political, and rhetorical use for the genre of poetry that celebrated—and helped to secure—the rights of workers.

They Wrote?

In approaching this forgotten body of labor poetry in the 1930s, it helps to begin by asking where it fits into the long tradition of working-class poetry in the United States, especially as that tradition began to compete with other—including mass and popular—cultures of the first decades of the twentieth century.

As long as workers have earned wages, worked under compulsion, or tried to form unions, they have tended to compose songs and poems about their experience. In his groundbreaking anthology, *American Labor Songs of the Nineteenth Century* (1975), Phillip Foner credits the first organization of workers in the United States, the Federal Society of Journeymen Cordwainers of Philadelphia, formed by Philadelphia shoemakers in 1791, for also producing what he calls "the first trade union song in American history": "Address to the Journeyman Cordwainers of Philadelphia," which emerged from the Cordwainers' 1799 strike against scab labor and a reduction in wages (11). And over the next century or so, Lowell mill girls, slaves, Knights of Labor, miners, Socialists, and Wobblies all composed songs and poems that reflected—and oftentimes inspired—working-class dissent and resistance.[6]

For many historians of labor culture, however, labor poetry of the 1930s does not follow in an unbroken line from the workers' poetry and song that preceded it, but instead remains an unexpected and therefore largely un-looked-for development—which may explain why, in addition to the legacy of the Cold War and the New Critics, even historians of labor culture and critics interested in the literary 1930s have rarely discussed this tradition of poetry. Indeed, many scholars seem to have assumed that when the working, living, and cultural conditions that enabled the production and distribution of nineteenth-century song-poetry ceased to exist, the labor song-poem sub-culture ceased to exist as well. In the conclusion to *Democracy, Workers, and God,* for example, his otherwise remarkable study of the nineteenth-century labor song-poem, Clark D. Halker argues that "song-poetry declined measur-ably after 1900, never again to enjoy the level achieved in the Gilded Age" (193). Halker attributes this decline to the widespread repression against labor in the 1890s, the economic depression of 1893, and the AFL's more conserva-tive brand of business unionism, which held that workers should not try to re-place capitalism or wage labor with socialism—a frequent theme of worker-poets in the late nineteenth centry—but should instead concentrate on higher wages and lower hours. For Halker, these two causes for the decline of the labor song-poem—capitalist repression of unions and AFL business unionism—were joined by a third of equal if not more fundamental signifi-cance, "the rise of popular culture and the industry responsible for its pro-duction" (199). "As popular culture made inroads into [the movement cul-ture] environment," he concludes, "and popular music and literature enjoyed a wider and wider working-class audience willing to purchase the industry's latest wares," working-class writers would compose fewer and fewer songs and poems (200). "Throughout the nation," Halker concludes, "workers turned to products the popular culture industry offered as new forms of entertainment or as replacements for traditional indigenous forms" (201).

Halker's conclusions match those of the renowned early- and mid-twen-tieth-century folklorist George Korson, who in a series of influential books documented the "amazing vogue" "balladry attained . . . among the an-thracite mine workers" in the nineteenth and early twentieth centuries. Like Halker after him, Korson blamed mass and popular culture for the disappear-ance of his beloved "minstrels of the mine patch" (7). "Isolation of the mine patch, a semi-primitive plane of living, harsh working conditions, illiteracy, the need for amusement, and folk imagination—these factors," Korson observed in 1938, "produced anthracite folk lore" (7). In contrast, he mourned, "The spread of popular education, the newspaper, the automobile, the movies, and the radio—these have combined to standardize life in the anthracite region as elsewhere in the land. Undoubted blessings, they have nevertheless blighted the folk imagination and checked the growth of folklore. By removing the need for self-amusement, they have deprived the miner of his urge toward self-expression" (12).

For many cultural historians of the labor movement, then, the moment of song and poem composition by workers more or less passes with the nineteenth century, and the onset of modernity and the rise of mass and popular culture render the labor song-poem as obsolete as oil lamps and daguerreotypes. Why should workers create or even participate in labor culture when, as Halker puts it, they could turn "to boxing and baseball, vaudeville, burlesque, nickelodeons, movies, and amusement parks" (200–201)?[7]

Halker appears to borrow much of his critique of popular culture from the Frankfurt School, the group of pre- and post–World War II German thinkers and exiles who worried over the relation between capitalism, mass culture, and politics; so too Korson, who seems to anticipate that school of critical thought (note his use of the verb "standardize"). In other words, both Halker and Korson clearly regret that the rise of popular and mass culture rendered workers passive consumers of culture rather than active producers of it. Moreover, since the decades of the 1920s and, even more so, the 1930s, witnessed the greatest consolidation of popular and mass culture yet to occur in the United States, if one takes Halker and Korson at their word, one would expect to find little in the way of song or poetry during precisely those two decades—just sports fans and film star worshippers humming the latest radio jingles. Yet as the labor historian Lizabeth Cohen argues in *Making a New Deal*, her study of industrial workers in Chicago between 1919 and 1939, mass and popular culture of the 1930s enabled working-class solidarity as much as or even more than it impeded it—largely by breaking down the rigid ethnic (and thus linguistic) barriers between workers. "The Polish and Bohemian worker laboring side by side at a factory bench," Cohen observes, "were now living much more similar lives than they had in 1919. Not only were they more likely to speak English, but they also could talk about seeing the same motion pictures, hearing the same radio shows, and buying the same brand-name products from the same chain stores. They also shared problems about the job that, even more important, they had begun to solve together, not just within their own ethnic work enclaves as in 1919" (211). "Ironically," Cohen later concludes, diverging from the traditional claims of labor historians, "the broader dissemination of commercial culture that accompanied its consolidation in the 1930s may have done more to create an integrated working-class culture than a classless American one" (357). In other words, not only could one listen to the radio *and* make a new deal in the 1930s, but those actions might mutually reinforce each other.

Moreover, one could listen to the radio, make a new deal—and, what is important for our purposes—write labor poetry about all of it. Indeed, one poem in this collection, "Ford Sunday Evening Hour," by an anonymous poet affiliated with the United Auto Workers, dramatizes just that method of composition. Still, that is not to say that organizers and worker-poets did not share Halker's and Korson's concern for the pacifying effects of mass and popular culture; as the anonymous poet of "Ford Sunday Evening Hour" demonstrates, they most certainly did. It is to say, however, that when organizers and worker-poets worried about mass and popular culture in the 1930s, they sometimes wrote poems about it. Further, to the extent that mass and popular cultures brought workers together, as Cohen argues, it also enabled the "turbulent" political and labor movements that inspired the labor poets in this collection. Even when mass and popular culture did not inspire poetry, then, it did not seemingly impede its production either. This collection does not incorporate any material from the first three decades of the twentieth century, but there is evidence to suggest that while the Depression decade did witness an "up-surge of creative activity," it did not witness a literal revival of that creative activity. In other words, if one looked closely at decades before the 1930s, one would probably discover that the production of labor poetry and song never died.[8] Thus while we owe these historians of labor culture an enormous debt for their work recovering the song-poetry of earlier periods, that research may have unintentionally contributed to the continued obscurity of later poetry by workers.

At the very least, Halker and Korson exaggerate the effect mass and popular culture had on the production of poetry and song by workers. Indeed, just tallying up the numbers is revealing. Halker observes that in the period between 1865 and 1895, "hundreds, if not thousands" of worker-poets "yielded several thousand song-poems" (2). In the period between 1929 and 1941, however—that is, in about one-third the number of years—at least as many worker-poets yielded perhaps just as many songs and poems in hundreds of union publications across the country. Moreover, these songs and poems are not the product of a professional cadre of composers, as Halker elsewhere charges, but the compositions of workers and organizers who seem just as "indigenous" and anonymous as nineteenth-century song-poets.

In contrast to the antimodern misgivings of early- and late-twentieth-century historians of labor culture, all the evidence points to the fact that working-class poetry (and song) continued to function throughout the twentieth century as a working-class cultural practice.

What They Wrote

Having survived the advent of mass and popular culture, what sort of topics did these worker-poets in the 1930s address? We have already noted that many of them worried about the same rise and potential influence of mass and popular cultures lamented by Korson and Halker, and oftentimes with just as much anxiety and unease as those two scholars. In addition to addressing the effects mass and popular forms like radio, comic strips, vaudeville, and films might have on working-class consciousness, however, worker-poets also treated the experience of *work* in the new mass and popular culture industries, whether the work of producing the hardware that made such culture possible (United Electrical, Radio, and Machine Workers of America) or the work of providing content for that culture (the American Federation of Musicians, the Associated Actors and Artistes of America). Here, for example, is Ann Winthrop cleverly describing the lot of the unemployed Broadway actor:

> I'm utterly and completely bored
> With the theatre; and starving for my art.
> It's come to the point where I just can't afford,
> To wait any longer for a part.
> Somewhere in this land of milk and honey,
> There must be a practical solution.
> I wonder if there would be any money,
> In starting a one-man revolution?

In addition to the occasional poem about mass and popular culture and the occasional poem—like Winthrop's—about work in the mass and popular cultural industries, many labor poems during the 1930s address what we might consider the more perennial themes of poetry. A few poems—especially those from the International Ladies Garment Workers Union and the Brotherhood of Sleeping Car Porters—celebrate nature in the pastoral tradition of American and British romantic poets. As with many of those poets, worker-poets often seem to turn to nature because of its distance from industrial capitalism, especially, as in the case of the garment workers or miners, because nature offers release and in many ways redemption from the confined and stifling space of the urban sweatshop or the underground mine.

Many worker-poets also composed poems in the tradition of what the ancient Greeks called encomia—that is, poems that praised a person's achievements and character, though instead of specific persons, worker-poets often chose to praise "labor" more generally (and thus to establish labor's claim to fair treatment and a decent wage) or to celebrate the accomplishments and victories of a given union. As Martin A. Dillman put it in his spirited poem dedicated to Waitresses' Union No. 249 and published in the *Catering Industry Employee*:

> Our Waitresses' Union—its equals are few,
> Has shown to the world what a Union can do!
> It marches right on in defense of its rights;
> Gosh! how those girls do win their court fights!
> It succors its members at home and at work,
> Then when a fight comes, no duty they shirk!
> This Local loves peace, yet it's never afraid;
> I take off my hat to the fight it has made!

In a similar celebratory vein, as throughout the nineteenth century, worker-poets often turned the traditional elegy—that is, the expression of grief on the occasion of a person's death—into what we might call the labor elegy. In these labor elegies, poets memorialized workers who died either through natural causes or in the course of their oftentimes dangerous work; they also mourned workers who died at the hands of the state or their employers, whether en masse (as sometimes happened in strikes) or singly, as in the long list of labor's executed or imprisoned martyrs. Indeed, the labor elegy occurs far more frequently in the pages of union newspapers than is included in this anthology. Nevertheless, Billy H. Quinn's "The Fatal Gilberton Mine," from the *United Mine Workers Journal,* represents the tradition well, as does Willie Sue Blagden's "To the Seamen of the International Brigades," which celebrates those—including Harry Hines, the editor of the International Seamen's Union newspaper *The Pilot*—who died defending republican Spain from the Fascists during the Spanish Civil War.

Despite Blagden's and other poems that celebrate the cause of Spain and those who defended it (as in "Madrid," Robert Whittaker's Industrial Workers of the World poem included here), worker-poets were far more likely to regret rather than to celebrate those who died in war, a regret that often inspired an outright denunciation of all war. These poets did not lack for opportunities to announce that antiwar position, either, since in the course of the 1930s Europe, Asia, and Africa all devolved into corpse-strewn battlefields. By the middle of the decade, Italy under Mussolini had invaded and conquered Ethiopia. Franco, with the help of Germany and Italy, defeated the republican government in Spain after three years of horribly violent civil war. Meanwhile, in Asia, Japan invaded mainland China, killing hundreds of thousands of Chinese peasants in a period of weeks. Back in Europe, Hitler annexed Austria, captured Czechoslovakia, overran Poland and the Netherlands, and, at the beginning of 1940, invaded and occupied France.[9]

Still smarting from the death, profiteering, and seemingly pointless conclusion of World War I, a majority of workers in the United States remained deeply opposed to involving themselves in another European war. Workers and their families concluded that as in World War I, they would do the bulk of the fighting and dying and receive little in return. Workers also feared that another war would distract from the problems of unemployment and housing at home, as well as roll back what economic gains they had managed to achieve in the second half of the 1930s. As the "poet laureate" of the United Electrical, Radio, and Machine Workers Union, Walter Mugford, put it in "Never Again":

Four years fought I for England's fame,
Thinking the Kaiser was to blame.
Dreaming poor fool, the blood of me
Was shed to spare democracy.
For what fought we? A nation's pride?
Why have those brave boys fought and died?
Through dripping bayonets, mud, and lice,
God, what a turmoil: What a price.

"Let labor learn such wars are vain," Mugford concludes: "Then we may live in peace again." To be sure, after Japan bombed Pearl Harbor and Germany declared war on the United States, many of these poets changed their stance toward the war. Prior to that, however, they built one of the sharpest bodies of antiwar poetry in the country's history.

Closely related to this broad, now mostly forgotten antiwar poetry is what we have now learned to call the "poetry of witness"—that is, poetry that seeks to document the extreme suffering of human beings in order to combat the very human tendency to forget such extremity and suffering.[10] The Great Depression, of course, created suffering on an enormous scale—unemployment, poverty, even starvation—and poets oftentimes sought to provide witness and thus remembrance of that suffering. Examples abound in the collection that follows, but the first stanza of Ruth Lechner's "If This Be My Native Land," published prominently in the newspaper of the United Rubber Workers, perhaps best represents that mood:

> If this be my native land, I am not proud,
> For mirrored in the searching pools that plunge
> And pry into the villages and towns,
> Are weak and hungry faces, gaunt and streaked
> With lines of rain. These are my people,
> And I am bitter with their sorrow.
> These are my people—and I am not proud.

Not satisfied with simply witnessing such suffering, many poets—especially those affiliated with the openly revolutionary Industrial Workers of the World—used poetry to inveigh against the economic system of capitalism that they believed represented the source of this inequality and suffering.

But we could not for long keep up a distinction between the poetry of witness (even the poetry of revolution) and easily the most frequent—and perhaps the most expected—themes of labor poetry in the 1930s: work, working conditions, and the struggle to improve those conditions. Indeed, the poetry of work in this collection provides bracing glimpses into the conditions that characterized many industries during the first half of the twentieth century. Miriam Tane, for example, poet and later organizer for the International Ladies Garment Workers Union, offered this description of the lives of Manhattan seamstresses:

> Soft, folded body
> forms an acute
> angle to sewing machine,
> and from tensioned limbs
> leap movements minutely
> calculated, hoarded from
> defeating time.

And as the void of listless
day widens into release
of night, the inert become
catapulting crowds seeking
the swift-running course
to the boroughs. Tide of
the going and the coming
is harnessed to the subway.
The days are similar as
one grain of salt to
another, and tomorrow is
formless to them who hate
what they are, yet have no
breath to sigh for what
they are not.

Tane's workers circulate to and from the alienating, soul-devouring machines of the sweatshop via the alienating, instrumental machine of the subway—a journey that does not even leave them with enough energy to regret their alienated, soul-devoured, instrumental lives. And just as Tane described the conditions of sweatshop workers, so too would other poets describe the special sorts of hell that characterized their own work: the desperation of the "shape-up" on shipping docks, the crushing pace of the automobile assembly line, the dangers and degradations of the coal mine, and, in any industry or craft, the fear of being laid off.

An anonymous poet for the Southern Tenants Farmers Union also described the wretched working and living conditions of sharecroppers. Instead of the merely pacifying and soul-destroying trap of work and subway rides sketched by Tane, however, this poet presented his readers, as he also titled his poem, with a "Share-Cropper's Choice":

Up early in the morning,
Only a bite to eat,
Mostly Bread and Molasses
Never a bite of meat.
Plowing long rows of cotton
Till noon bell calls to eat
Bean-soup, bread, and molasses
Never a bite of meat.

> Plowing in evening sunshine
> Tired, too darned tired to eat
> Beans, Corn-bread, and molasses
> But it's that _____ or organize.

As "Share-Cropper's Choice" suggests, and as we might gather from a collection of poetry originally published in newspapers of established or incipient unions, many poets did not stop with merely describing the harrowing conditions of their work, but described what happened—the difficulties as well as the successes—when workers made the "choice" to organize and to try to improve their lives. By far the most popular poem of the labor movement, for example, "The Label Tells a Story," a version of which sooner or later appeared in almost every AFL, CIO, and unaffiliated union newspaper, urged workers to practice solidarity not just as workers but as consumers as well:

> You're a union member I take it, for you pay your union dues
> But my friend, is there a label of a union in your shoes?
> Do you see the union label on the tobacco that you buy?
> Or upon the newspaper you read?
> You can get it, if you try.

The majority of these sorts of poems, however, focused on organizing on the shop floor, at the point of production rather than consumption. A poet who identified himself only as a "Canadian Ford Worker" offered this representative injunction to his fellow autoworkers:

> To my American brothers,
> And democracy lovers,
> I jot down a rhyme
> On company time.
>
> To make some contribution
> To industrial revolution,
> And help sound the knell
> Of industrial hell,
>
> We must without fear—
> Our duty is clear—
> Together put a stop
> To the last open shop.

Before they could sound the knell of industrial hell, however, workers and organizers encountered many barriers that made the always difficult task of organizing even more difficult. Prior to and even after passage of the Wagner Act, for example, which nominally outlawed them, many employers started "company unions" that sometimes offered workers life insurance and other perks but which nevertheless remained powerless—or worse, detrimental—when it came to issues like wages, working hours, or the speedup. In order for workers to establish their own unions, they oftentimes had to discredit—or take over—preexisting, ineffectual company unions, and many poems aided in that effort.

In addition to company unions, however, workers and organizers had to confront employers whose commitment to "the open shop" (that is, a non-union shop) remained fierce and who as a result marshaled all possible force—including their own and, in some cases, that of the state—against union movements. During the campaign to organize Ford workers, for example, the Dearborn city council, at Henry Ford's request, outlawed leafleting, and police arrested organizers who violated that law; ex-boxers and criminals on the Ford payroll also routinely beat up UAW organizers, most famously at the Battle of the Overpass, when photographers captured one particularly brutal beating on film.[11] Before they capitulated at Flint, too, General Motors employed what a 1936 congressional committee called "the most colossal supersystem of spies yet devised in any American corporation" in order to infiltrate unions and fire workers who either organized or expressed sympathy for the union. By documenting such abuses—for these specific examples from the UAW, see Murray Roth's two poems "Dearborn Hospitality" and "A Stoolie's Lament"—worker-poets underscored the depravity of employers and thus the virtue of the union movement.

Of course not all the poems in this anthology fall neatly into one of these categories, and many poems draw from several categories at once, but they nevertheless provide us with a rough guide to the content and modes of workers' poetry in labor newspapers. In addition to this variety of content, however, labor poetry of the 1930s—as even the brief survey above suggests—relied on a variety of forms as well. To be sure, most worker-poets chose to use thoroughly standard—even conventional—forms. In other words, their poems usually rhyme, and, though often inventive, imagistic, satiric, and even ironic, they nevertheless strive to remain as accessible as possible to as many readers as possible.

Exceptions to these conventional formal rules, however, abound. The United Auto Workers' pseudonymous Poll, for example, wrote long, free verse poems that, with their nonstandard capitalization and short, heavily enjambed lines, clearly betray the influence of the modernist revolution in poetic form. Miriam Tane, whose work is quoted above, expresses her contempt for the sweatshop specifically and modern life more generally through a sort of imagistic, at times metaphysical free verse that frequently relies on allusions to popular culture and the detritus of the consumer economy. However, the most unusual worker-poet in terms of form and, perhaps, even content, has to be the pseudonymous Mr. Modestus, who published in a number of labor newspapers—the Musicians, the Textile Workers, the Ladies Garment Workers—throughout the 1930s. Like Poll, Mr. Modestus wrote long, free verse poems, yet his poems discursively wind their way from geography to statistics to philosophical speculation and back again—oftentimes building to quite remarkable insights about work and life in the 1930s. Few poets between the wars—or since—have used this form to such effect.

Still, most of the poems included in this anthology—and most of the poems published in union newspapers not included in this anthology—do in fact follow fairly conventional forms. For academic readers still trained in New Critical and modernist poetic sensibilities, which usually value free verse and difficulty over rhyme and accessibility, that conventionality can pose a problem, perhaps even lead them to dismiss this poetry as mere propaganda—as did a whole generation of literary critics. Yet we have to remember that those New Critical poetic prejudices were neither universal nor universally accepted; rather, they have a very specific history. If we ignore the contingency of those beliefs about poetry, we risk anachronistically bringing them to bear on worker-poets who did not share their premises.

Indeed, we should remember that worker-poets had good reasons to choose the forms they did, not just that they failed to hear the news about T. S. Eliot, Cleanth Brooks, and the poetry of the ironic fragment. For one, many worker-poets—and many of their readers—would have had some familiarity with the history of labor poetry and song-poetry in the nineteenth and early twentieth centuries. Those poets oftentimes composed lyrics to be sung—and thus employed that venerable crib of memorization, rhyme; and so worker-poets in the 1930s quite sensibly borrowed that technique for poems that they too wanted workers to, if not memorize or sing, at least remember. As for today, too, most workers encounter poetry in the form of songs on the radio—almost all of which use rhyme. Indeed, one of the songs autoworkers composed and sang during the Flint sit-down strike, "The Fisher Strike," borrowed its tune from a country-and-western song, Gene Autry's "The Martins and the Coys," then quite popular on the radio. It should not surprise us, then, that when workers turned to writing their own poems, they imagined participating in these ready-to-hand poetic and popular poetic traditions and not the relatively new and relatively obscure modernist poetic tradition of the 1910s and 1920s.

Why They Wrote

But workers chose these standard and conventional forms not simply because they knew them best but because they fit their purpose, which brings us to the question of why they wrote these poems at all. In his remarkable study *Poetry and the Public,* Joseph Harrington describes a tradition of public poetry, especially active in the first decades of the twentieth century, which "understood poetry to engage and intervene in public life" (17). In contrast, high modernist poets and critics displaced this public-oriented view of poetry with their own "private," now dominant view of poetry, one that valued the poem as an aesthetic object in and for itself and as a way for its poet and its reader to escape the debased mass, popular, and sentimental cultures—including the mass, popular, and sentimental poetic cultures. In contrast, public poetry, as Harrington documents, "was meant to serve a public, often social, function" (17) and to act "as a vehicle or mode for participating in and engaging with the public" (11). As Mark W. Van Wienen describes this tradition, in the context of politically committed poets who responded to World War I through newspaper verse, "The norm for poetry writing—and, at least in certain respects, the ideal—was not high art but journalism" (6). Public poets thus "reversed conventional expectations about what poetry is supposed to accomplish: not the achievement of timelessness, of carving out a place in the canon of great literature, but the impact of timeliness, influencing historical and political conditions here and now" (6).

For the most part, worker-poets belong to this tradition of public and journalistic poetry, and so it of course influenced the forms they chose. In order for poetry to serve that social, even journalistic function, it had to remain accessible to its public readers. And while when they composed and submitted their poems for publication they usually had a more specific public in mind than poets publishing in mass circulation newspapers—not the public per se, but their fellow workers and fellow (or potential) union sympathizers—they still wished to influence those reader-workers, to engage them, to persuade them, to, as Horace put it, instruct and delight them. As we have seen, they wanted to instruct and delight them about politics, about war, about suffering, about their own working conditions, about the perfidy of their employers, and about "the choice" they had and should make to improve their lives. The poets chose conventional forms, then, because they suited their rhetorical and political aims—not because they were bad poets.

In retrospect, of course, we can question the efficacy of their choice of forms and their poetic and political project, if not necessarily the reasons why they made those formal choices. After all, poetry, as W. H. Auden put it, "makes nothing happen,"[12] a conclusion that would seem to undercut both the aims of public poetry and thus the poetic forms employed to advance those aims. One of the many things to admire about this body of workers' poetry, however, may be the answer it implies to this problem. In contrast to those critics, even poets, who sometimes overestimate how much culture and literature can affect the political realm, these poems seem to reconcile themselves to Auden's pessimism. Perhaps because they appeared in newspapers devoted to maintaining or establishing unions, and because their authors oftentimes functioned as not just de facto but as actual organizers, the poets included in this anthology seem to recognize that poetry, by itself, could not make a union or, as in the case of the IWW, a revolution. By themselves, these poems seem to say, poems do not form unions; they do not stop bullets or dissipate tear gas; they will not slow down the assembly line; and they will not get you your job back if your foreman lays you off. Henry Ford did not read the poetry published in the *United Auto Worker* and realize the error of his thug and tear-gas ways.

Indeed, instead of apologizing for its political incapacity and abandoning culture altogether, workers' poetry of the 1930s—and in other periods as well— makes the most of what poetry can do. Together, these poems seem to recognize that organizing workers into unions does not require poems per se, but it does require what the labor historian David Montgomery calls a militant minority: "the men and women who endeavored to weld their workmates and neighbors into a self-aware and purposeful working class" (2). And though they may not do much else, poems can contribute some of the rhetorical heat necessary to weld workmates and neighbors together. To say that poetry by itself *makes* nothing happen, then, is not to say that poetry *does* nothing. Indeed, Auden's line underestimates what poetry can do, and so it underestimates what I believe 1930s poetry by workers did manage to do. And that is to remind workers of the old IWW preamble that "the working-class and the employing class have nothing in common," an aphorism that while doubtlessly reductive is nevertheless absolutely necessary for the exercise of working-class power (qtd. in Kornbluh 12). As the contemporary labor economist Michael

Zweig puts it, "To exercise power you need to know who you are. You also need to know who your adversary is, the target in the conflict. When the working class disappears into the middle class, workers lose a vital piece of their identity. In political, social, and cultural terms, they don't know who they are anymore" (74). If they did nothing else, then, these poems reminded people who they were and who their adversaries were. They were workers, sped-up and abused, and their adversaries were their employers, who, when it came down to it, would just as soon throw them in jail and fire tear gas or guns at them as raise their wages or allow organizers to help them form a union. Far from causing us to despair about the efficacy of political poetry, then, the cultural and political pragmatism these poems manifest should only add to their value and to these poets' accomplishment. They remind us that poetry specifically and culture more broadly can make something happen, but only when allied with an active, collective political or social movement.

If so, then we might harbor some misgivings about recovering these poems in their present context. On the one hand, the repression of political poetry—including poetry written by and about workers during the 1930s— has done considerable damage to our understanding of the field of modern American poetry. It has similarly damaged our understanding of the variety of social forms and functions poetry occupied during that period—and could occupy in our own. On those grounds alone, these poems deserve recovery and study. As Cary Nelson argues in *Repression and Recovery*, "For texts previously ignored or belittled, our greatest appreciative act may be to give them fresh opportunities for an influential life" (14); those texts "can gain that new life," he continues, "in part through an effort to understand what cultural work [they] may have been able to do in an earlier time" (11). By gathering and reproducing these poems into this anthology, I have tried to aid just that understanding of these poems' cultural work, as well as to aid an understanding of poetry that sought to *do* cultural and political work in the first place.

Yet if these poems and worker-poets find a new audience today, they will mostly find it within universities, whether among scholars or students, and while that does not rob them of their political and cultural meaning, it does alter it somewhat. These poems were written for workers, most of them by workers, and published in working-class newspapers. Conceived rhetorically, their success and their value depended upon delighting, instructing, and converting their audiences, who were not academics or students, but (again) workers. If they succeed in delighting their newfound contemporary readers and instructing them of the history of working-class organization, the role poetry played in it, the necessity for it today, and the courage required of it in the face of its ongoing adversaries, so much the better. Nevertheless, my perhaps naive but nevertheless real hope is that these poems might delight and instruct the contemporary counterparts to their original audiences—that is, workers today. Similarly, that they might inspire new poetry, poetry that would both emerge from and inspire new movements for workers' rights and livelihoods. If they did, then they might again accomplish what they once managed to accomplish: aiding in the creation of a self-aware and purposeful, even "turbulent" working class, prepared to meet the new forms of economic turbulence that linger and that seem to gather more force every day.

Organization and Methodology

I have chosen to arrange the poems that follow according to the union publication in which they appeared, instead of by poet or by date of publication. There are many reasons to do so, not least of which is that most of the worker-poets in this collection imagined writing and speaking to members or potential members of their union in the context of other poems and other material to appear in those publications. Within the sections devoted to a union, I have arranged the poems chronologically.

I have also divided the collection into three sections according to the affiliations of the individual unions—that is, whether a given union belonged to the American Federation of Labor, the Congress of Industrial Organization, or had no or only brief affiliation with either of those bodies. Though such a division risks reproducing the uncomplicated belief in a "conservative" AFL and a "radical" CIO, a belief that many of the poems and poets in this collection seriously call into question, the division nevertheless reflects the historical sweep of the decade. For the first half of the 1930s, the AFL predominated; when it failed to take the lead in organizing unskilled and semiskilled workers in the new, mass production industries, only then did the CIO displace the AFL as the leading actor in the ranks of organized labor.

For only a very few poets have I tried—and for even fewer have I succeeded—in tracking down biographical information. Fearing reprisals from their employers, many poets chose to write anonymously or to adopt pseudonyms. Unfortunately, that strategy also makes it extraordinarily difficult for later readers of this poetry to learn anything about these poets' biographies. For poets whose names we do know, however, it nevertheless proved a daunting task to discover biographical details about them; it also seemed like partly a pointless one, though, since many of the original readers of these poems valued them because of what they said, what they reflected, and what they made possible—not because of *who* wrote them, except of course that they were written by someone like them, someone of their own class, indeed of their own industry, union, even city or factory.

That said, if readers take an interest in these poems, they will undoubtedly take an interest in the people who wrote them. Therefore, whenever I have been able to discover something about a poet, I have given that information in a footnote. I offer these biographical details, though, with the following caveat, which is that they are unavoidably skewed toward poets who, for one reason or another, went on to lead lives sufficiently public that it later became possible for me to learn something about them. In other words, we should not assume that these poets tell us much at all about the other poets in this collection—especially the many who published anonymously or under pseudonyms.

In lieu of extensive biographical information about the poets, I have written brief introductions to the unions in whose newspapers the poems appeared and, when appropriate, introduced some of the history or culture of the workers who labored in the industry or craft covered by the union. For these introductions, I have relied on two works: Gary M. Fink's *Labor Unions* (1977) and the outstanding edited collection, *Who Built America: Working People and the Nation's Economy, Politics, Culture, and Society* (1992). In order to keep the introductions relatively uncluttered, I have not cited these sources. I hope that readers understand such a decision not as an attempt to pass off this long-in-the-making and valuable research as my own, but to present the fruits of it as clearly and conveniently as possible.

For many of the poems, I have provided footnotes that explain the oftentimes esoteric details of working conditions and practices in a given industry or craft, the political controversies of the decade, or the local labor battles of a given union—all of which the authors of these poems rightly assumed their local and immediate readers would understand but which their later and perhaps unimagined readers might not.

Finally, I will say a word about methodology. Given what I have argued about the continuity of labor poetry across the early decades of the twentieth century, the opening and closing dates for this collection deserve comment. While I would have liked to produce an anthology of labor poetry that encompassed the first half of the twentieth century, or even the whole of the twentieth century, such a project would have taken closer to a lifetime rather than the few years this one did. So I have chosen to restrict the anthology to the period between 1929 and 1941, for several reasons. The onset of the Great Depression in late 1929 introduced unimaginable suffering into the lives of many workers, unlike anything most of them had ever experienced before. At the same time, it also offered historic opportunities for those workers to improve their lives, especially in the context of a federal government that eventually came to recognize workers' right to organize and then compelled employers to recognize that right as well. Not surprisingly, this suffering, paired with these opportunities, inspired many workers to join unions, and many of those to write poetry. Moreover, the Great Depression and the labor movement that arose in its wake also provided workers with an unprecedented outlet for that poetry. Nearly every union published a monthly or bimonthly newspaper in the 1930s. These newspapers and their editors not only accepted workers' contributions and made space for them, but in most cases actively encouraged workers to submit their work. To some degree, these conditions—this suffering and these opportunities, this movement and these newspapers—obtained before the Great Depression, but never in such a concentrated form, and never, I would hold, to such literary effect.

This unique historic interlude, however, largely comes to an end with the Japanese bombing of Pearl Harbor in 1941. The crises of World War II resuscitated the ailing U.S. industrial economy, mitigating much of the suffering of the Great Depression by raising wages and, especially as men were drafted into the army and as industry recovered, by giving work to the staggering number of unemployed. The war also ushered in a whole new set of labor relations. Most unions signed—and most workers supported that decision—no-strike clauses in order to guarantee the flow of material necessary for the conduct of the war; in return, and because they really had no choice, most employers treated their workers more decently than they ever had. Most of the large companies that had successfully fought off the CIO during the 1930s—the Ford Motor Company, for example—were compelled, under the threat of losing war contracts from the federal government or losing production during those boom years, to recognize their workers' unions. With some exceptions, then, the breathtaking labor battles of the 1930s came to an end. From now on, workers and organizers could start a union by voting for one, not necessarily by forming a picket line, sitting down in a factory, or getting arrested, beaten, or murdered by hired goons and the local police. Without more evidence, we cannot say for certain what effects these developments brought on by the war in reality had, but from the survey I have made of the war period, they seem to have lessened the desire—and the overwhelming need—for workers to write poetry. But we have been wrong about these sorts of things before.

Second, I was fortunate to do the bulk of this research at the University of Illinois at Urbana-Champaign, one of a handful of universities in the country that have made a systematic attempt to gather and to preserve (or at least not to discard) the hundreds of periodicals that emerged from the labor movement in the United States. In assembling this collection, I consulted almost every CIO journal from October 24, 1929, to December 7, 1941; so too the "unaffiliated" unions of the Industrial Workers of the World, the Southern Tenants Farmers Union, and the International Seamen's Union; as well as every major American Federation of Labor craft union. Limits on my energy, my time, and the University of Illinois collection, however, prevented me from consulting all of the many, oftentimes quite small AFL or unaffiliated unions. So while I make no claims to have exhausted this enormous archive, I believe I can confidently claim to have fairly represented it.

I have not been able to determine why a given union (the Teamsters, for example) did not publish poems while other unions did, though it doubtless depended upon a number of interrelated and perhaps inextricable factors: the size of the union, the activity and militancy of the union, the desire of its members to write poetry, a tradition of poetry within that industry, craft, or union, and, finally, the willingness or reluctance of editors of the newspapers to publish poetry.

Finally, since I only include a few more than 150 of the thousands of poems uncovered in the course of my research, I ought to say a word about how I have selected them. Quite simply—or perhaps not simply at all—I have chosen what I considered to be the most historically revealing, the most inventive, and the most indigenous of the published poems. By "indigenous" I mean poems written by workers, members of workers' families, or organizers with ties to the union, in contrast to the many famous and then-famous poets—like Lord Tennyson, Edgar Guest, and Ella Wheeler Wilcox—that union newspapers, especially unions affiliated with the American Federation of Labor, frequently reprinted, sometimes to fill space. While these poems might tell us a great deal about the taste of editors and perhaps of workers, they remain available elsewhere and rarely reveal much about workers or the unions themselves.

Even after ruling out those reprinted poems, however, thousands remained, and I have opted, as I indicate above, for the most historically revealing and the most formally inventive. To be sure, this mode of selection sacrifices some of the force of the argument advanced above—that is, that traditional criteria of poetic value like "imaginative" and "inventive" should not overly determine our estimation of these poems' rhetorical and cultural work, which exists somewhat independently of their aesthetic value. Nevertheless, arguing that evaluation is always a contingent, historical process does not mean that some poems did not realize their rhetorical, cultural, political, and poetic aims better than others. And it is those poems that seem best fitted for winning this remarkable body of poetry the audience it deserves.

Notes

1. See Irving Bernstein, *Turbulent Years*.

2. I borrow much of the discussion of the "turbulent" 1930s in this and following paragraphs from Freeman et al., *Who Built America,* specifically the two chapters "The Great Depression and the First New Deal" and "Labor Democratizes America."

3. Many writers, who already shared these commitments or came to share them, enlisted (sometimes literally) in the cause. Internationally, Americans—including, perhaps most famously, the poet Edwin Rolfe—volunteered to help Spanish Republicans defeat General Francisco Franco's German and Italian-backed fascists in the Spanish Civil War, while the novelist Ernest Hemingway volunteered to cover the war for the North American Newspaper Alliance and to raise funds for it in the United States. At home, Communists and their allies organized in support of the Scottsboro Boys, and many artists and poets (Langston Hughes foremost among them) rallied to their defense. Finally, and perhaps most influentially, the Popular Front inspired a cultural front of novelists, poets, playwrights, filmmakers, screenwriters, and singers who would, as their leading historian has characterized it, orchestrate the "laboring" of American popular culture during the second half of the 1930s (Denning, *Cultural Front,* xvii).

4. Some of the best-known anthologies that appeared slightly before or during the 1930s include Manuel Gomez's *Poems for Workers;* Marcus Graham's *Anthology of Revolutionary Poetry* (1929); Granville Hicks's *Proletarian Literature in the United States: An Anthology* (1935); *We Gather Strength* (1933); and Alan Calmer's *Get Organized: Stories and Poems about Trade Union People* (1939). Later anthologies include Joyce Kornbluh's *Rebel Voices: An IWW Anthology* (1964); Jack Salzman and Barry Wallenstein's *Years of Protest: A Collection of American Writing of the 1930s* (1967); Alan Lomax's *Hard Hitting Songs for Hard Hit People* (1967); Walter Lowenfels's *The Writing on the Wall: 108 American Poems of Protest* (1969); Aaron Kramer's *On Freedom's Side: An Anthology of American Poems of Protest* (1972); and Jack Salzman and Leo Zanderer's *Social Poetry of the 1930s: A Selection* (1978). Among the few critical works that appeared are Walter Rideout's *Radical Novel in the United States, 1900–1954* (1956), Daniel Aaron's *Writers on the Left: Episodes in American Literary Communism* (1961), and Marcus Klein's *Foreigners: The Making of American Literature, 1900–1940* (1981).

The last two decades, however, have seen a wealth of new scholarship on the 1930s and labor literary culture more generally. See especially Rita Barnard, *The Great Depression and the Culture of Abundance* (1995); Constance Coiner, *Better Red: The Writing and Resistance of Tillie Olsen and Meridel Le Sueur* (1995); Michael Davidson, *Ghostlier Demarcations* (1997); Michael Denning, *Mechanic Accents* (1987) and *The Cultural Front* (1996); Alan Filreis, *Modernism from Left to Right* (1994); Barbara Foley, *Radical Representations* (1993); Laura Hapke, *Labor's Text* (2001); Joseph Harrington, *Poetry and the Public* (2002); Walter Kalaidjian, *American Culture between the Wars* (1993); Sherry Linkon and Bill Mullen, eds., *Radical Representations: Rereading 1930s Culture* (1996); William J. Maxwell, *New Negro, Old Left* (1999); Charlotte Nekola and Paula Rabinowitz, eds., *Writing Red: An Anthology of American Women Writers, 1930–1940* (1987); Cary Nelson, *Repression and Recovery: Modern American Poetry and the Politics of Cultural Memory, 1910–1945* (1987) and *Revolutionary Memory: Recovering the Poetry of the American Left* (2001); Paula Rabinowitz, *Labor and Desire: Women's Revolutionary Fiction in Depression America* (1991); Robert Shulman, *The Power of Political Art* (2000); Michael Thurston, *Making Something Happen: Partisan Political Poetry in the U.S. between the Wars* (2001); Alan Wald, *Exiles from a Future Time: The Forging of the Mid–Twentieth Century Literary Left* (2002). In terms of recent anthologies, Paul Lauter and Ann Fitzgerald's *Literature, Class, and Culture* encourages its readers to view working-class and other literary texts through the lens of class; John Graham's *"Yours for the Revolution": The* Appeal to Reason, *1895–1922* (1990) gathers decades' worth of articles, cartoons, stories, and poems from the leading socialist newspaper in the United States; Nicholas Coles and Peter Oresick's anthologies *Working Classics: Poems on Industrial Life* (1990) and *For a Living: The Poetry of Work* (1995) collect contemporary working-class poetry; Cary Nelson's *Modern American Poetry* devotes significant space to left-wing and radical poets throughout the twentieth century; finally, Nicholas Coles and Janet Zandy have recently published *American Working-Class Literature: An Anthology* (2007).

5. Karyn Hollis's "Material of Desire: Bodily Rhetoric in Working Women's Poetry at the Bryn Mawr Summer School, 1921–1938" is a notable exception, as are Colette A. Hyman's "Politics Meet Popular Entertainment in the Workers' Theatre of the 1930s" and Michael Denning's discussion of the ILGWU-sponsored musical *Pins and Needles* in *Cultural Front*. Cary Nelson's *Revolutionary Memory* discusses poems and poem-cards to emerge from the early-twentieth-century labor movement. Two additional works deserve mention here, too: *Rhyme and Reason: Molders Poetry from Sylvis to the Great Depression* (1984), edited by James E. Cebula and James E. Wolfe, and a more recent book, David Duke's *Writers and Miners: Activism and Imagery in America* (2002). Finally, one might mention Robert S. McElvaine's excellent collection, *Down and Out in the Great Depression: Letters from the Forgotten Man* (1983).

6. "In the main," Foner summarizes this poetry, "the songs and ballads in the labor papers dealt with the organizations and struggles of working people, their hatred for their oppressor, their affirmation of the dignity and worth of labor, their determination to endure hardships together and to fight together for a better life" (xiv). "They provide us," he concludes, "with insights into the causes of strikes and other labor issues from the viewpoint of workers themselves, and they indicate what the composers—themselves often participants in the struggles—thought would be the most stirring way to mobilize workers" (xv).

7. To be fair, Halker allows that "song-poetry can hardly be described as a dead letter after 1900" and that "a revival of sorts took place in the [twentieth] century and in a re-organized labor movement" (194). Be that as it may, Halker does not think much of this revival. "With the possible exception of the Industrial Workers of the World," he argues, "at no time after 1900 did as many individuals contribute song-poems as in previous decades" and that, correspondingly, "fewer labor papers and journals published after 1900 included song-poems in their pages; those that did rarely printed them as a regular feature" (194). Moreover, after 1920, "as in many activities associated with the labor movement," "professionalism crept into the song-poet's craft," and instead of a broad, indigenous movement, "a small number of individuals wrote the majority of songs" (194).

8. For a start, and in addition to the many AFL newspapers published during this period, one might look at the song and poetic practices of the various radical political parties and unions, including the many publications of the Socialist Party, most notably *Appeal to Reason,* and, of course, the publications and circulars of the prolific Industrial Workers of the World. Moreover, and though it presents more of a challenge, in many urban areas workers from similar ethnic backgrounds maintained their own fraternal organizations, out of which came newspapers published in their native language, many of which likely contain much original poetry.

9. For an accessible overview of the diplomatic and military history of the people, see David M. Kennedy's *Freedom from Fear.*

10. On the poetry of witness, see Carolyn Forche's remarkable anthology, *Against Forgetting: Twentieth Century Poetry of Witness* (1993).

11. For oral histories of this period provided by Ford workers themselves, see Stepan-Norris and Zeitlin's *Talking Union.*

12. I borrow this phrase from Auden, of course, but also from Michael Thurston's study *Making Something Happen.*

Bibliography

Aaron, Daniel. *Writers on the Left: Episodes in American Literary Communism.* New York: Avon, 1961.

Abrams, M. H. "Poetry, Theories of (Western)." *The New Princeton Encyclopedia of Poetry and Poetics.* Princeton, NJ: Princeton UP, 1993.

Auden, W. H. "In Memory of W.B. Yeats." *The Norton Anthology of English Literature.* Eds. M. H. Abrams et al. Vol. 2. New York: Norton, 1993.

Barnard, Rita. *The Great Depression and the Culture of Abundance.* Cambridge: Cambridge UP, 1995.

Bernstein, Charles. *The Turbulent Years: A History of the American Worker, 1933–1941.* Boston: Houghton Mifflin, 1969.

Brooks, Cleanth. *Modern Poetry and the Tradition.* Chapel Hill: U of North Carolina P, 1939.

Calmer, Alan. *Get Organized: Stories and Poems about Trade Union People.* New York: International Publishers, 1939.

Cebula, James E., and James E. Wolfe, eds. *Rhyme and Reason: Molders Poetry from Sylvis to the Great Depression.* Cincinnati: Sylvis P, 1984.

Cohen, Lizabeth. *Making a New Deal: Industrial Workers in Chicago, 1919–1939.* Cambridge: Cambridge UP, 1990.

Coiner, Constance. *Better Red: The Writing and Resistance of Tillie Olsen and Meridel Le Sueur.* Urbana: U of Illinois P, 1998.

Coles, Nicholas, and Peter Oresick, eds. *For a Living: The Poetry of Work.* Urbana: U of Illinois P, 1995.

Coles, Nicholas, and Janet Zandy, eds. *American Working-Class Literature: An Anthology.* New York: Oxford UP, 2007.

Davidson, Michael. *Ghostlier Demarcations: Modern Poetry and the Material Word.* Berkeley and Los Angeles: U of California P, 1997.

Denning, Michael. *The Cultural Front: The Laboring of American Culture in the Twentieth Century.* London: Verso, 1997.

Denning, Michael. *Mechanic Accents: Dime Novels and Working-Class Culture in America.* London: Verso, 1998.

Duke, David C. *Writers and Miners: Activism and Imagery in America.* Lexington: UP of Kentucky, 2002.

Filreis, Alan. *Modernism from Left to Right: The Thirties and Literary Radicalism.* Cambridge: Cambridge UP, 1994.

Fink, Gary M., ed. *Labor Unions.* Westport, CO.: Greenwood P, 1977.

"The Fisher Strike." *United Auto Worker,* January 1937, 7.

Foley, Barbara. *Radical Representations: Politics and Form in U.S. Proletarian Fiction, 1929–1941.* Durham, NC: Duke University Press, 1993.

Foner, Philip. *American Labor Songs of the Nineteenth Century.* Urbana: U of Illinois P, 1975.

Forché, Carolyn, ed. *Against Forgetting: Twentieth-Century Poetry of Witness.* New York: Norton, 1993.

Hicks, Granville, et al., eds. *Proletarian Literature in the United States: An Anthology.* New York: International Publishers, 1935.

Freeman, Joshua, et al., eds. *Who Built America: Working People and the Nation's Economy, Politics, Culture, and Society.* Vol. 2: *From the Gilded Age to the Present.* New York: Pantheon, 1992.

Gomez, Manual. *Poems for Workers.* Chicago: Daily Worker Publishing, n.d.

Graham, John, ed. *"Yours for the Revolution": The Appeal to Reason, 1895–1922.* Lincoln, NE: U of Nebraska P, 1990.

Graham, Marcus. *Anthology of Revolutionary Poetry.* New York: Active P, 1929.

Halker, Clark D. *For Democracy, Workers, and God: Labor Song-Poems and Labor Protest, 1865–1895.* Urbana: U of Illinois P, 1991.

Hapke, Laura. *Labor's Text: The Worker in American Fiction.* New Brunswick, NJ: Rutgers UP, 2001.

Harrington, Joseph. *Poetry and the Public: The Social Form of Modern U.S. Poetics.* Middletown, CO: Wesleyan UP, 2002.

Hollis, Karyn. "Material of Desire: Bodily Rhetoric in Working Women's Poetry at the

Bryn Mawr Summer School, 1921–1938." *Rhetorical Bodies*. Ed. Jack Selzer and Sharon Crowley. Madison: U of Wisconsin P, 1999.

Hyman, Colette A. "Politics Meet Popular Entertainment in the Worker Theatre of the 1930s." *Radical Revisions: Rereading 1930s Culture*. Ed. Sherry Linkon and Bill Mullen. Urbana: U of Illinois P, 1996.

Kalaidjian, Walter. *American Culture between the Wars: Revolutionary Modernism and Postmodern Critique*. New York: Columbia UP, 1993.

Kennedy, David. *Freedom from Fear: The American People in Depression and War, 1929–1945*. New York: Oxford UP, 1999.

Klein, Marcus. *Foreigners: The Making of American Literature, 1900–1940*. Chicago: U of Chicago P, 1981.

Kornbluh, Joyce, ed. *Rebel Voices: An IWW Anthology*. Ann Arbor: U of Michigan P, 1964.

Korson, George. *Minstrels of the Mine Patch: Songs and Stories of the Anthracite Industry*. Hatboro, PA: Folklore Associates, 1964.

Kramer, Aaron, ed. *On Freedom's Side: An Anthology of American Poems of Protest*. New York: Macmillan, 1972.

Lauter, Paul, and Ann Fitzgerald, eds. *Literature, Class, and Culture*. New York: Longman, 2001.

Linkon, Sherry, and Bill Mullen, eds. *Radical Revisions: Rereading 1930s Culture*. Urbana: U of Illinois P, 1996.

Lomax, Alan. *Hard Hitting Songs for Hard Hit People*. New York: Oak Publications, 1967.

Lowenfels, Walter, ed. *The Writing on the Wall: 108 American Poems of Protest*. Garden City, NY: Doubleday, 1969.

Maxwell, William J. *New Negro, Old Left: African American Writing and Communism between the Wars*. New York: Columbia UP, 1999.

McElvaine, Robert S. *Down and Out in the Great Depression: Letters from the Forgotten Man*. Chapel Hill: U of North Carolina P, 1983.

Montgomery, David. *The Fall of the House of Labor: The Workplace, the State, and American Labor Activism, 1865–1925*. Cambridge: Cambridge UP, 1987.

Nekola, Charlotte, and Paula Rabinowitz, eds. *Writing Red: An Anthology of American Women Writers, 1930–1940*. New York: Feminist P at the City University of New York, 1987.

Nelson, Cary, ed. *Anthology of Modern American Poetry*. New York: Oxford, 2001.

Nelson, Cary. *Repression and Recovery: Modern American Poetry and the Politics of Cultural Memory, 1910–1945*. Madison: U of Wisconsin P, 1989.

Nelson, Cary. *Revolutionary Memory: Recovering the Poetry of the American Left*. New York: Routledge, 2001.

Oresick, Peter, and Nicholas Coles, eds. *Working Classics: Poems on Industrial Life*. Urbana: U of Illinois P, 1990.

Rabinowitz, Paula. *Labor and Desire: Women's Revolutionary Fiction in Depression America*. Chapel Hill: University of North Carolina Press, 1991.

Rideout, Walter. *The Radical Novel in the United States, 1900–1954: Some Interrelations of Literature and Society*. Cambridge: Harvard UP, 1956.

Salzman, Jack, and Barry Wallenstein, eds. *Years of Protest: A Collection of American Writings of the 1930s*. New York: Pegasus, 1967.

Salzman, Jack, and Leo Zanderer, eds. *Social Poetry of the 1930s: A Selection.* New York: B. Franklin, 1978.

Shulman, Robert. *The Power of Political Art: The 1930s Literary Left Reconsidered.* Chapel Hill: U of North Carolina P, 2000.

Spector, Herman, et al. *We Gather Strength: Poems.* New York: Liberal P, 1933.

Stepan-Norris, Judith, and Maurice Zeitlin, eds. *Talking Union.* Urbana: U of Illinois P, 1996.

"Strike Songs: Battle, Victory, Joy." *United Auto Worker,* January 1937, 7.

Thurston, Michael. *Making Something Happen: Partisan Political Poetry in the U.S. between the Wars.* Chapel Hill: U of North Carolina P, 2001.

Van Wienan, Mark W. *Rendezvous with Death: American Poems of the Great War.* Urbana: U of Illinois P, 2002.

Wald, Alan. *Exiles from a Future Time: The Forging of the Mid–Twentieth Century Literary Left.* Chapel Hill: U of North Carolina P, 2002.

Zweig, Michael. *The Working-Class Majority: America's Best Kept Secret.* Ithaca, NY: ILR P, 2000.

PART I

American Federation of Labor

American Federation of Musicians

Professional musicians began forming trade unions as early as the 1860s and in 1896 founded the more permanent American Federation of Musicians, which steadily gathered members throughout the first three decades of the twentieth century. The union even managed to weather the storms of Prohibition and the Great Depression, which closed nightclubs where many musicians worked. More fatal than either of those very real threats, though, was the advent of sound motion pictures ("talkies") and of recorded (or "canned") music, which eliminated thousands of jobs in silent movie theaters and threatened the livelihood of "live" performers everywhere. Both of these threats found their way into the poetry musicians published in their union newspaper, *The Musician,* including the conspiratorial fantasy "The Wizard of Robot," which imagines a world where mechanization has led to mass unemployment and, as a result, imperiled the mechanized industries themselves.

Weirdly, *The Musician* also published the work of "Mr. Modestus," whose distinctively long, discursive poems would appear in other labor newspapers throughout the 1930s, including those of the Industrial Workers of the World, the United Textile Workers, and the International Ladies Garment Workers Union. The first of the poems reprinted here, "Men are asking for work," explores the difference between what the British poet and reformer William Morris called "useful work" and "useless toil." "Adventure," in turn, considers not just how the Great Depression disrupted the economy but, even more seriously, how that failing economy may have permanently disrupted people's habits, practices, even their understanding of themselves.

The Wizard of Robot

Gertrude Munter

Pooh Bah Ben Dahmem, may his tribe decrease,
Awoke one night from a dream of peace,
He mused as he lay in his great ornate room
How he'd send all his fellowmen straight to their doom!
He stretched out his hand, while he chortled with glee
And pressed all his buzzers, "Come here quick," yelled he.
For they knew if they didn't, he'd surely raise_____.
"Get all my electricians, wherever they may be,
And have them report mighty pronto to me!

Get carpenters, builders, yes, architects, too;
I've thought of a job that I've got to put through!
I've made up my mind a wizard I'll be
And tie up all business but just what suits me.
I've decided the world I'll control with one hand,
By the press of a button, I'll millions command!"
So they rushed out and gathered a motley array
Of experts quite clever for this King for a Day.
They pondered and puzzled for over a year
Till his wonderful scheme was perfectly clear.

Then he set out his henchmen all over the world;
In each city bought buildings and his banner unfurled.
They wired all the buildings straight into his room,
Where he chuckled at planning the workingman's doom.
Each building was turned into a theatre grand,
And covered with lights that illumined the land;
And filled with great Robots that moved at his touch,
(That laborers would suffer did not trouble him much)
And the ones who had helped him, when their work was done,
Were dismissed just as if they had never begun.

Then came the great day, when his work was complete,
And he sat back complacent in his overstuffed seat.
Each theatre had robots from doorman to roof,
Cashiers and ushers were strictly fireproof.
The pictures were radioed right onto screen,
With music from somewhere entirely unseen.
The organ would groan and the tin horns would shriek,
All at the touch of this crazy old Sheik.
Then came the grand opening! He pressed on the switch
And all the doors opened with nary a hitch.

The cashiers sat nodding, cosmetics on tin,
The doorman stood waiting for folks to come in.
The ushers all ready to walk down the aisle,
But not a one ever could crack up a smile.
The horns were dispensing their horrible sound;
Everything worked in his Merry-Go-Round!
But Alas and Alack, the magnets he bought
Were none of them human, just simply Robot!
While the people he'd figured their money they'd spend,
Were all of them workmen who had come to their end!

So, sadly he waited for dough to roll in
Through the hands of his cashiers all covered with tin,
Till he fell down stone dead with a terrible bang.
The doctors all said, "'Twas a plain Boomerang!"
Now this is the end of this horrible tale.
Musicians, buck up, your fate don't bewail.
The end is in sight of our awful old fix!
Old Pooh Bah was crazy, the ROBOT IS NIX!

From The Musician, *May 1930. Compare Leigh Hunt's "Abou Ben Adhem," which begins "Abou Ben Adhem (may his tribe increase!)" Hunt's poem goes on to suggest that God blesses those who love their fellow men.*

Men are asking for work
Mr. Modestus

Men are asking for work
But who really wants to work?
Many of these men need food for their families.
They are willing to sell their labor to get it.
But do any of them really want to labor?

There is such a thing as the habit of work, the habitual use faculties.
There is also such a thing as a purpose to be attained by work.
To let the natural powers be idle too long, is to lose them.
Not to gain the end desired—takes meaning out of life.
Yes, there are men who really want to work.

A carpenter, who keeps his tools clean and sharp;
Who can work to a line, and can fit a miter joint that needs no putty.
A blacksmith who really can shoe a horse; a mechanic who knows his
        motors—
There might even happen to be an engineer in the chain gang—
And he would rather make a good job of the road.
A structural steel worker—risking his life in a gale on a cable.
A Paderewski[1]—willing to pay the price of his musical power.
A Michelangelo[2]—willing to "mix brains with his paints."
Men will die—have died—for the chance to do creative work.

Some statesmen work—put their lives to it.
George Norris[3]—and the "lame duck" amendment to the constitution.
No President of the United States but accepts the task of his job, open-eyed.

---

1. Ignacy Paderewski, Polish pianist, composer, and later statesman whose 1891–92 tour of the United States turned him into a celebrated and revered musician among American audiences.
2. Michelangelo Buonarroti, Italian sculptor, painter, architect, and poet in fifteenth- and sixteenth-century Italy.
3. George Norris, congressman and senator who, during the 1930s, sponsored a series of landmark pieces of progressive legislation, including the Norris-LaGuardia Act, which forbid the use of judicial injunctions in labor disputes, the bill that created the Tennessee Valley Authority, and the Twentieth Amendment to the Constitution, which moved the inauguration date for presidents and congressmen to January instead of March, thereby reducing the amount of time when "lame duck" defeated officials continued to exercise power in Congress.

A Briand[4]—brokenhearted, for the great work unfinished.
Some of these sell themselves into veritable slavery—and do it eagerly.

Change the question, then—
What man just wants to labor?
What man would not prefer leisure?
Labor—for the sake of just living?
Labor—the grind—the collar—just to keep alive?
Toil—drudgery—mere carrying of bricks and hammering of iron:
To just plod—with no goal?
To roll ever up the hill, the rock that inexorably shoves you down again?[5]
The men who rebelled at that, have been history-makers.
They have been the pioneers, who went down into the unknown, rather
    than submit to chains.

You can put these two things together—and men will laugh at them.
Real men—and women—will take up toil as blessing—
If it opens the door to the goal.
Mothers—mothers of men—have ever smiled, and carried the heavier end,
    for nothing but love.
Men—who have been counted useless else—have faced the chain gang as a
    sacrifice.
Inventors, artists, visionaries, explorers, missionaries—
No extremity of toil and test of endurance has been too great.

But there was a goal, there was a call, there was a star—a heaven to gain.

But men have guts enough—will refuse to stay alive—just to carry a chain.

From The Musician, *May 1932. Mr. Modestus's poems were published without titles in a col-*
umn entitled "Riding at Anchor." For convenience, the first line of each poem is given for the
title.

---

4. Aristide Briand, French statesman and leader of the country during World War I. After
the war, Briand emerged as a leading international peace advocate.
5. In Greek mythology, Sisyphus was condemned to push a heavy rock to the top of a steep
hill, where it would always roll down again.

Adventure

Mr. Modestus

Adventure—
That is, a turning toward—something—
It means, a venture—an uncertainty.
Excursion—
That is, a going out of—
And a moving away from,
Wherever you have been up to now.
Adventure, excursion—
That has been happening to America—
For the last five years.

Release from old surroundings—
Cutting off old associations—
Original decisions—made upon demand of new conditions—
Actions outside the realm of old habits.
Compulsion of strange forces—
Facing of untried possibilities—
All of this has come to the American people,
Since the Great Depression—
Came around the corner.

Concerning four million families—
Is the adventure, the excursion—
Especially and most forcefully true.
The four million families who are on "relief"—
Are testing the sensations of new sets of conditions.
Old habits of "making a living"—
Habits of "keeping up with the Joneses"—
Habits of housekeeping, and of clothing—
Habits of working—or of not working—
Money-habits—giving way to money-less habits—
Habits that go with "these things are mine"—
Giving way to other habits of "glad to have anything"—
Habits of using the hands—
Of lifting, and pushing, and cutting, and fitting—

Habits of looking, or watching, or listening, or feeling—
Useful habits once—for holding your job—
Habits almost forgotten now—
How good it would feel to get back into them—
Like the feel of an old shoe—even if it pinched somewhere—
These habits are all getting flabby—
They don't hold in place anymore—
Although they used to be in control—
They could be depended upon to carry through—
If one was a little tired, or off-color.

These are the skill-habits—
From which mechanics have been taking excursions—
The service-habits, from which we have been adventuring.
Millions of us have almost lost the old habits—
Which enabled us to fit into the places where we lived.
There used to be 75,000 mechanics—
Working in the machine-tool manufactures.
Today, there are not enough of them to meet demand.
They have been adventuring—
Off on excursions—riding freight trains, thumbing their way—
There is work for them now—
But they don't come back.

What new habits do you suppose their adventures have formed?

From The Musician, *November 1934.*

American Federation of Teachers

Founded in 1916, the American Federation of Teachers was slow to attract members and, like most AFL unions, lost what members it did have during the antiunion 1920s. But also like most AFL unions, the American Federation of Teachers grew exponentially in the 1930s, especially in cities, where it managed to improve working conditions and, in some states, to pass limited teacher tenure laws. Not surprisingly, the poetry published in the union's *American Teacher* reflects an interest in education: in "Just Another Day," the bureaucratic responsibilities of schooling interfere with teaching, and in "Amos 'n Andy," mass communication, far from enabling mass education, actually disseminates mindless (even racist) drivel.

Just Another Day
Nell Owen, Local 52

Keep up your faith, O teacher!
Be not bowed down in sorrow;
You were not allowed to teach today
But maybe you'll be tomorrow!

You stand before your classes in the freshness of the morning
With your very best to give them and all lesser efforts scorning.
There is perfect contact with them, they are working hard—no capers,
When a lady lightly enters, in her arms a stack of papers.

"I have come to give your pupils a little mental test;
You will grade the finished papers but I will do the rest.
And we will thank you at the office if you will kindly hurry
With so many schools to hear from, you've no idea what a worry."

And out she trips and leaves you with your shattered senses reeling
While visions of the mound of themes that always wait come stealing.
You take a grip upon yourself, start in once more—no matter.
A messenger comes banging in with dreadful noise and clatter.

"The nurse says send her all your boys!" The Three R's, once so treasured,
Are forced to take a back seat while the boys are weighed and measured.
No use proceeding with the lesson, no use becoming vexed,
Since the period is wasted for the girls will go out next.

When that at length is over, and with a long sigh of relief
You begin the reading lesson, O. Henry's "Ransom of Red Chief."
It's a thing they all delight in, with appreciative giggles;
You mark the progress of their reading by the current of their wiggles.

Just as you think you're making headway
The dentist sends for Arthur Treadway.
The spell is broken, the mood is gone;
Unlike his thrush, you can't recapture
Browning's "first, fine careless rapture;"[1]
The rest is only plodding on.
Wearily you take another book
As the dentist calls for Mary Cook.

You rally in the afternoon, resolved at last to do or die,
You begin with composition and the pupils really try.
There is peace at least ten minutes, when at the principal's command,
A wingless Mercury[2] appears with a paper in his hand.

Announcement of the meeting of the Civic Club next night
Must be written on the board so each child will get it right.

---

1. From Robert Browning's "Home Thoughts from Abroad": "That's the wise thrush; he sings each song twice over, / Lest you should think he never could recapture / That first, fine careless rapture" (14–16).
2. In Roman mythology, the messenger of the gods.

With that at last accomplished and the work begun again,
Comes a tiny lisping tot, "Hath anybody theen my pen?"

Next a grinning pupil enters with a note, you stop to see,
And read the brief announcement: "Orchestra practice is at three."

A visitor gives a timid knock,
And so it goes till three o'clock.
Came the dawn: the morning papers,
This flaming legend bore:
"Teacher placed in straight-jacket,
Beats head upon the floor."

Place me on Sunium's marbled steep,[3]
Surround me with the ocean deep;
Put a class within my reach,
And then, good Lord, just let me teach!

From The American Teacher, *April 1931.*

---

3. From Lord Byron's *Don Juan:* "Place me on Sunium's marbled steep, / Where nothing save the waves and I, / May hear our mutual murmurs sweep; / There, swan-like, let me sing and die" (Canto III, Stanza 86).

Amos 'n Andy

E. H. H. Holman

The scientist worked with his tubes and his tools;
   He probed nature's secrets and learned its deep rules;
He weighted distant stars and he harnessed light;
   He studied the atom, too small for man's sight;
He taught the electrons to fly through the air;
   Discerning, he wrought with great labor and great care.

Behold his great gift as the radio sings
   And the voice leaps the distance as though it had wings.
"What voice," you may ask, "do we get every night?"
   "Whose voice rides the ether waves bringing delight?"

No Plato or Keats or the wise men of earth;
   But a pair of white "coons" with mechanical mirth.
For of all the broadcasters in the whole race
   It's Amos 'n Andy[1] who hold the first place.

From The American Teacher, *April 1931.*

---

1. In 1928 *Amos n' Andy* became the first serial radio program. It recounted the adventures of two African Americans from rural Georgia as they came north to find work in Chicago. The show, the creation of two white vaudeville actors, Freeman Gosden and Charles Correll, borrowed many of its conventions and humor from the blackface minstrel tradition, including outrageous situations and bad puns, but also that tradition's demeaning stereotypes of African Americans. The formula was enormously popular, and by 1931 roughly forty million Americans regularly listened to the nightly broadcast.

Associated Actors and Artistes of America

Though the Associated Actors and Artistes of America can trace its origins back to protective unions formed in the nineteenth century, its history really begins in 1919 with the merger of two independent, Manhattan-based unions, the White Rats Actors Union of America and the Actors' Equity Association. Later that year, after an organization of theatrical producers sought to break the union, the AAAA called a strike, which lasted for less than a month but which nevertheless resulted in recognition of the union as sole bargaining agent and substantial gains for actors, including the right to negotiate over salaries, working conditions, travel expenses, and employment security.

Still, the poetry the union published in its journal, *Equity,* reveals that not even these organizing successes could mitigate the everyday indignities and insecurities of making a living on the stage, especially during the Great Depression, when many theaters closed. "Revenge without Music," for example, is one actors' fantasy of exacting heavenly revenge on cruelly indifferent theatrical agents. "Reverie" is a comic reflection on the schemes unemployment and starvation will inspire—in this case, the slightly ironic one of starting a revolution in the hopes of making money. Another *Equity* poem, "Don't Bite the Hand," is unique in this collection (and in the labor poetry from this period more generally) in that it questions whether traditional forms of direct or collective action will really work, especially in the world of theater, where neither a revolution, a picket line, nor a sit-down strike can help struggling, less-than-highly-talented actors when there are no jobs to be had, let alone improved. "Questionnaire for Actors," finally, offers an imagined conversation between two unemployed actors in order to dramatize the hardships they face in the 1930s.

Revenge without Music

Peter Donald, Jr.

Through all this jostling Broadway mob
I wend my weary way.
I'm searching for a steady job,
At reasonable pay.
But, everywhere I go, I find
The agent says, "Oh no!
But *I'll* try to keep *you* in mind,
And I will let you know."
From Pitman's to the Sardi place
I tramp with footsteps slow.
But Signor Paley scans my face,
And sighs, "I'll let you know."
So onward to Fifth Avenue
To Briscoe's lair I go.[1]
And he says, "No, there's naught for you.
Still I will let you know."
Oh, someday I will leave this life,
And soar into the blue.
I'll get a job in Heaven. Strife
Can have no more to do;
For I'll stand within the Pearly Gates
And tell souls where to go.
But when the agents ask their fates,
I'll leer, "I'LL LET YOU KNOW!!"

From Equity, *September 1936. Peter Donald, Jr. (1893–1978?), appeared in various Broadway plays during the 1930s. He had a minor part (Johnnie Sparks), for example, in the 1934 production of* The Pure at Heart, *by left-wing stage and film writer John Howard Lawson.*

---

1. Pitman, Sardi, Paley, and Briscoe were all prominent Broadway theatrical agents during the 1930s.

Reverie

Ann Winthrop

I'm utterly and completely bored
With the theatre; and starving for my art.
It's come to the point where I just can't afford,
To wait any longer for a part.
Somewhere in this land of milk and honey,
There must be a practical solution.
I wonder if there would be any money,
In starting a one man revolution?

From Equity, *December 1936. Like Peter Donald, Jr., Ann Winthrop (1902–1982) made various Broadway appearances. She played Ann Harmon in the 1936 production of Philip Wood and Stuart Beach's* Lend Me Your Ears *and Ruby Keefer in the 1933–34 production of Courtney Burr's long-running comedy* Sailor, Beware.

Don't Bite the Hand

Lee Willoughby

Strike, strike, strike,
   Actor and Artist and Clerk,
What do they know what it's like
   To be *all* the time without work?

Where can *I* picket today?
   The law of the jobless to live?
The whole of the length of Broadway?
   Because I have nothing to give?

Because as an actress I'm fair
   But never could really be great
Can I picket a job that's not there?
   Can I fight against ultimate fate?

What use if I sat on a floor?[1]
  'Twas a floor never mine to begin.
What good if I rant and I roar?
  And what have I got if I win?

The chance to do something I can't,
  A principle won at a price.
A victory won with a rant,
  And a job that I couldn't hold twice?

Why strike against something you've got!
  When so many have nothing—I say
That maybe it isn't a lot
  But I'd take it—and gladly, today.

I'd kneel and I'd render my thanks
  For the smallest of chances, no more,
But you'd never find me in the ranks
  Of the people who sit on the floor.

From Equity, *January 1937.*

---

1. Given the date of the poem, this is almost certainly a reference to the January 1937 UAW sit-down strike at the General Motors factory in Flint, Michigan.

Questionnaire for Actors

Frances Scanlin

1. When did you last eat?
  (Or don't you know?)
2. Have you landed a part?
  (Or aren't you the type?)
3. When do you start rehearsals?
  (Or do you?)
4. How do you like the notices?
  (Who does?)
5. Have you had your screen test?
  (What did it cost you?)

6. What happened to the play?
   (Oh, was it a play?)
7. Did you see me in Hamlet?
   (Was that you? tch-tch!)
8. How come *you're* not working?
   (Who is, except the WPA?)[1]
9. Did you pass the ERB?[2]
   (Yes, but he didn't speak.)
10. Do you know anyone who's casting?
    (Do you?)
11. Who's your agent now?
    (What would I pay him with?)
12. When did you eat last?
    (I've forgotten.)
13. How come you're not working?
    (Me work? I'm an actor.)
14. What do you intend to do about it?
    (How do I know?)

From Equity, *January 1937.*

---

1. The Works Progress Administration, a relief measure established in 1935 and designed to provide work for the unemployed. It included the Federal Theatre Project, which provided funding for unemployed actors and sponsored plays that toured the country and brought stage drama to many communities.
2. The Emergency Relief Bureau, an early New Deal program later connected to the Federal Theatre Project. In order to be eligible, applicants had to pass a test establishing financial need.

Brotherhood of Maintenance of Way Employes

Since 1892, the Brotherhood of Maintenance of Way Employes represented workers across the United States and Canada who built and repaired railroad tracks and bridges. An extremely active, proud, and literary union, the Brotherhood went so far as to wonder in a July 1936 editorial whether the Depression would "create a new crop and new type of 'hobo poetry.'" While not exactly hobo poetry, a great deal of poetry was published by the Brotherhood of Maintenance of Way Employes, perhaps more than by any other comparable AFL union. What follows is a mere sample.

Begging for Bread

Thomas R. Lynch

Begging for bread—in a plentiful land!
  Begging for bread—with a trade in his hand!
Sound as a dollar, in heart and in head,
  Ready for work, and yet—begging for bread!

Begging for bread—but not begging alone;
  Now they are swollen to numbers unknown,
Who weary the highways with heart-breaking tread,
  And swarm through our city streets—begging for bread.

Begging for bread—with such stores on our hands
  We could feed the unfed of all habited lands;

Food rotted to order—starvation widespread—[1]
  Organized waste—millions—begging for bread!

Begging for bread—while dividends still
  Choke the fat coffers and bulge Dives's till![2]
"Coming-out parties" increasing their spread
  And blessed in their name who are—begging for bread!

Chief of the Nation today on the air,
  And all the big talkers—with language to spare—
Urging the half poor, already well bled—
  To save our prosperity—begging for bread![3]

From The Railway Maintenance of Way Employes Journal, *April 1931.*

---

1. In the spring of 1933, the Agricultural Adjustment Administration paid farmers to plow up roughly ten million acres of cotton and to slaughter six million baby pigs; prior to that, other states enforced various crop reduction schemes. For more on these polices, see the note to Covington Hall's "Surpluses, O the Surpluses!"
2. In Luke 16:19-31, Jesus offers the parable of the rich man, Dives, and Lazarus, a beggar whom Dives refuses even the scraps from his table. In the afterlife, Lazarus goes to heaven while Dives suffers in hell.
3. In a 1932 radio address, Herbert Hoover blamed the Depression on the "individual American" hoarding currency. See William E. Patton's "The Sin of Hoarding" for excerpts from that speech.

Working Mother's Prayer

Edna Jacques

God keep her safe, she is so small to leave,
In empty rooms, to fret and watch and grieve,
With only make-believe and dolls to play;
It is too cold to let her out today.
And I have need to earn our daily bread,
And hold my job, that we may still be fed.

Oh "give Thine Angels charge"[1]—a little one
Who left us here before her play was done,
She might be glad to come to earth once more
And play with blocks upon a sunny floor,
And dress her dolls and play her favorite game,
And keep her company until I came.

And when it's warm and she can play outside,
Let them go out along the pavements wide,
Down to the park to swing and feed the swan
And hunt for four-leaf clover on the lawn.
And help her watch at corners of the street,
Those buses are so swift for little feet.

I shall not mind the long hours if I know,
Someone is there wherever she might go,
Holding a hand before her childish face—
Walking with her along a dangerous place—
And when I turn the corner I may see
Her watching there upon the steps for me!

From The Brotherhood of Maintenance of Way Employes Journal, *January 1932. The poem was accompanied by the following note from the editor: "This poem was written by a Saskatchewan woman and sent in by Judge Emily F. Murphy."*

---

1. From St. Augustine's "Evening Prayer": "Watch Thou, O Lord, / with those who wake, / or watch, or / weep tonight, / and give Thine angels / charge over those who sleep."

Company Unionism

Gequel

Come into our Company Union[1]
  Said the Spider to the Fly
It's the finest little Union
  That you ever did spy.
The cost to join is nothing;
  The things you get, the same.
It's like a regular Union
  Until you know the game.

There are no paid executives;
  Therefore, you pay no dues.
For officers, you may elect
  Just anyone you choose.
You meet in our nice office,
  The Company pays the freight;
The only thing we ask is that
  You seek no better rate.

The members must be loyal
  To the purpose of the game.
We seek to better dividends,
  But keep your rate the same.
You must shun outside Unions,
  And avoid the use of heads;
For those who do some thinking
  Are called Radicals or Reds.

---

1. In the 1920s, some large corporations set up company unions in order to win workers' loyalty and fend off outside unions. A staple of the newly theorized "welfare capitalism," these unions offered life insurance, recreational facilities, profit-sharing plans, and sometimes old-age pensions, but as unions they remained enthralled to the needs of management and rarely raised substantive issues of wages or working hours. In the 1930s, company unions also emerged as a way for corporations to adhere to section 7a of the National Industrial Recovery Act, which stated that "employees shall have the right to organize and bargain collectively through representatives of their own choosing," without having to sacrifice much in the way of authority or profit.

We hold our little meetings
  And decide your future fate;
But if you seek more wages,
  You are destined for the gate.
With our superior wisdom,
  We know what's best for you;
So worry not about your lot,
  We'll tell you what to do.

When speaking of the Company,
  You must say "we" and "us."
This makes you feel important,
  Although not worth a cuss.
We call you our "co-workers";
  You're as happy as can be,
If you stay away from Unions
  And just refuse to see.

From The Brotherhood of Maintenance of Way Employes Journal, *July 1936.*

Brotherhood of Sleeping Car Porters

In 1925, a group of Pullman porters, together with the assistance of African American leaders like the venerable A. Philip Randolph, organized the Brotherhood of Sleeping Car Porters. The union demanded that the Pullman Company, which owned and operated the nation's railroad cars, double porter's average wages, eliminate tipping, and limit working hours. From the start, however, the Pullman Company—as well as the Ku Klux Klan in the South— bitterly opposed the union, driving it underground until in 1936 it received a charter from the AFL and, taking advantage of the Wagner Act, signed its first contract. In later years, the Brotherhood of Sleeping Car Porters—its leaders and members—would play a key role in the civil rights movement.

Their poetry, published in *The Black Worker,* is represented here by "Stick, Boys!" which was written and published during the period when the union had gone underground and its prospects seemed bleak. "Discernment" and "Brighter Ash" are two poems firmly within the imagist tradition of the 1910s. Their presence—among other such imagist, haiku-like poems in the newspaper—suggests that *The Black Worker* occasionally functioned as a clearinghouse for all sorts of poetry, not just poetry about labor or the union.

Stick, Boys!

Bennie Smith

Are you sick of the game? Well, men that's a shame
You're young, and you're brave, and you're bright—
You've had a "raw deal," I know—but don't squeal,
Buck up, do your damnedest and fight.

It's the plugging away that will win you the day,
So don't be a quitter, old pard,
Just draw on your grit, it's so easy to quit,
It's to work for low wages that's hard.

It's easy to say that you're beaten and lie;
It's easy to crawfish and crawl;
But to stick and to fight, when hope seems out of sight,
Why that's the best man of them all.

Should you come out of each grueling bout
All broken and beaten and scarred,
Just continue to fight—It's dead easy to try
It's the long hours you are working that's hard.

From The Black Worker, *June 1930. Benjamin "Bennie" Smith was a founding officer of the Brotherhood of Sleeping Car Porters and later one of its several vice presidents. For more information on Smith, see Jervis Anderson's* A. Philip Randolph: A Biographical Portrait *(1986).*

Discernment

Aseneth Cargill

A white butterfly
Perfectly poised
Upon a cabbage leaf;
A jade carving
Flawless in workmanship—
Exquisite in design—
Discovered by discerning eyes
In a sunlit garden.

From The Black Worker, *June 1941.*

Brighter Ash

Anonymous

The woodbine's leaves are reddening now,
The sumac branch is tipped with fire.
Autumn is touching twig and bough.
The woodbine's leaves are reddening now,
While yellow, the arrowhead in sough
Burns brighter ash than burning Tyre.[1]
The woodbine's leaves are reddening now,
The sumac branch is tipped with fire.

From The Black Worker, *June 1941.*

1. An ancient Phoenician city on the eastern Mediterranean Sea in present-day Lebanon, it was besieged and captured by Alexander the Great in 332 B.C.

International Fur and Leather Workers Union

Though the Fur and Leather Workers Union has a long history dating back to 1849, it did not publish much original poetry during the 1930s. It is included in this collection in order to represent the many unions that reprinted one of the most common poems of the 1930s, "The Label Tells a Story," sometimes also called "The Union Label." At a moment when mass consumption first took hold in the United States, the poem urged workers to extend their labor sympathies beyond the factory floor and the sphere of production to the sphere of consumption, the newly established supermarkets and department stores.

The Label Tells a Story

Anonymous

You're a union member I take it, for you pay your union dues
But, my friend, is there a label of a union in your shoes?
Do you see the union label on the tobacco that you buy?
Or upon the newspaper that you read?
You can get it, if you try.

Is a label in the pocket of the suit upon your back?
A label on your collar, or a chinese spider track?[1]

---

1. This reference remains unclear, though it could refer to nonunion garments made under the sweating system, in which Chinese tailors might have been those most willing to work for the lowest wages.

Do you find the union label in the sweatband of your hat?
Look and see if you can find it—did you ever think of that?

How about the union label on brooms your wife swings?
How about it on your table or a thousand other things?
There's a moral in this poem; you can find it, if you try.
If at first you fail to see it, ask yourself the reason why.
Always be Union in everything you buy.

From Fur and Leather Workers Journal, *February 1941.*

Hotel and Restaurant Employees and Bartenders International Union

Organized in 1890, the Hotel and Restaurant Employees and Bartenders Union suffered from the start of Prohibition in 1920 and the subsequent decline in membership numbers. With the repeal of that law in 1933, however, together with a newfound commitment to organizing largely unskilled, mainly women restaurant workers, the union thrived during the 1930s. Like hundreds of poems that appeared in labor newspapers, "Waitresses' Union No. 249" catalogues and celebrates its officers and accomplishments. The following two poems, "A Square Deal or a 'Quare' Deal" and "Supreme Court," address national politics more than local union politics, but their irony underscores how much the latter depended upon the former—whether the NRA or the anti–New Deal decisions of the Supreme Court.

Waitresses' Union No. 249

Martin A. Dillman

Our Waitresses' Union—its equals are few,
Has shown to this world what a Union can do!
It marches right on in defense of its rights;
Gosh! how those girls do win their court fights!
It succors its members at home and at work,
Then when a fight comes, no duty they shirk!
This Local loves peace, yet it's never afraid;
I take off my hat to the fight it has made!

Our Waitresses' Union, with valor renown!
Remember those battles with places downtown?
Those winter-time pickets refused to say "lose."
Their feet nearly froze to the soles of their shoes!
Take a lesson from these and learn the "Why-When!"
Skat! Shut up your bragging, you egotist men!
This Local loves peace, yet it's never afraid;
I take off my hat to the fight it has made!

Kitty is Field Marshall and Viola keeps the books,
Yes, Mollie she's game, so look out, you big crooks!
That wide-awake Board has its foes beat a mile,
Backed up, as it is, by a loyal Rank and File!
Local 249, Whoop! I write this with pride,
May that cracker-jack bunch for a century abide!
This Local loves peace, yet it's never afraid;
I take off my hat to the fight it has made!

From The Catering Industry Employee, *August 1930. The poem was accompanied by the following note from the author: "Dedicated to the recent grand triumph of the Local 249 in the Steinberg Injunction suit.—M.A.D."*

A Square Deal or a "Quare" Deal

James M. Bishop, Local 34

The steel men are not feeling gay
They don't believe in the N.R.A.[1]
For why should they permit their men
To say what they'll work for; how and when?
It's simply outrageous to think that they
Should figure reductions in *their* pay,
And stock dividends, oh! my word!
To reduce them is, of course, absurd.
It is now just thirty years since
George F. Baer[2] made miners wince;
Told them, and the world, the Lord Himself,
Had placed the miners on a shelf;
Control of which, by Divine command,
Was placed in him and his chosen band.
Steel and oil, autos and coal,
Open-shoppers all swear by that pious role;
And this Divinely appointed band,
In their own way would "Save the land."

From The Catering Industry Employee, *December 1933.*

---

1. National Recovery Administration, one of the first New Deal programs. For each industry, including steel, the NRA outlined a series of voluntary codes regulating, among other things, working hours and minimum wages. Section 7a of the National Industrial Recovery Act, a linked piece of legislation, also stated that "employees shall have the right to organize and bargain collectively through representatives of their own choosing," though the act made no provisions for enforcing that right.
2. U.S. railroad magnate. During his tenure as head of the Philadelphia and Reading Railway Company, Baer represented coal mine owners during a 1902 strike in Pennsylvania. In an open letter to the press in August of that year, Baer wrote, with ill-considered paternalism, "The rights and interests of the laboring man will be protected and cared for, not by the labor agitators, but by the Christian men to whom God in his infinite wisdom has given control of the property interests of the country and upon the successful management of which so much depends."

Supreme Court

Anonymous

Nine old men in a white marble tomb
On the will of the people enunciate doom.

Nine old men who often divide,
Four to dissent, five to decide.

Nine old men who rise to defend
Property rights to the bitter end.

Nine old men by logical stages
Demolished the law for minimum wages.[1]

Nine old men whose bygone prattle
Condemned the Negro to be a chattel.[2]

The nine old men wax eloquent
On the holiness of six per cent.

Nine old men, senile and flighty,
But second only to God Almighty.

From The Catering Industry Employee, *April 1937.*

---

1. In *Adkins v. Children's Hospital* (1918), the Supreme Court ruled that minimum wage laws violated the Fifth Amendment and liberty of contract. Later, in *Morehead v. New York* (1936), the Court confirmed that ruling, declaring minimum wage laws a violation of freedom of contract.
2. In *Dred Scot v. Sanford* (1857), the Supreme Court decided that people of African ancestry could not become citizens of the United States and therefore could not sue in federal court; the Court also ruled that the federal government did not have the power to prohibit slavery in its territories. The "six per cent" allusion, in the following couplet, as yet remains unidentified, though it may refer to the traditional return on investments expected by holders of stock.

International Association of Machinists

In many ways, the International Association of Machinists is typical of AFL unions during the first half of the twentieth century. Born from the ashes of the Knights of Labor in the 1880s, deeply craft-conscious, occasionally racist, and frequently ambivalent toward strikes and its socialist past, the Machinists nevertheless grew and won gains for its members throughout the first decades of the twentieth century. Like other AFL unions, too, it suffered from the backlash of the 1920s, only to emerge again in the 1930s and attract new members. The poetry of the Machinists is in many ways typical too. Like other labor newspapers of predominantly male unions, *The Machinist* had a page devoted to what it imagined to be the concerns of women—recipes, fashion, and family health mostly. Those "women's pages" also regularly printed poetry, most of it devoted to sentimental evocations of home and motherhood, though occasionally, as in "The Ninety and Nine," the sentimentalism appeared to more openly political ends. Both "The Ninety and Nine" and "Surplus Value," however, also demonstrate how deeply even a crude version of the labor theory of value penetrated traditionally conservative AFL craft unions. Finally, "While Playing Santa Claus" is in the tradition of perhaps the most common labor poem of the 1930s, "The Union Label," which urged workers to buy only products made by union labor.

The Ninety and Nine

Rose Elizabeth Smith

There are ninety and nine that work and die,
In hunger and want and cold,
That one may revel in luxury,
And be lapped in the silken fold;
And ninety and nine in the hovels bare,
And one in a palace of riches rare.

From the sweat of their brow the desert blooms
And the forest before them falls;
Their labor has builded humble homes,
And the cities with lofty halls;
And the one owns the cities and houses and lands,
And the ninety and nine have empty hands.

But the night so dreary and dark and long
At last shall the morning bring;
And over the land the victor's song
Of the ninety and nine shall ring,
And echo afar, from zone to zone:
"Rejoice, for labor shall have its own."

From The Machinist Monthly Journal, *November 1931.*

Surplus Value
Anonymous

The merchant calls it profit,
  And he winks the other eye;
The banker calls it interest,
  And he heaves a cheerful sigh;

The landlord calls it rent,
  As he tucks it in his bag;
But the good honest burglar
  Just simply calls it "swag."

From The Machinist Monthly Journal, *June 1935.*

While Playing Santa Claus
Thomas H. West

'Twas nearing Christmas, down the street
  Mazuma[1] in his jeans,
A union man went sauntering,
  Enjoying all the scenes.
He was a thrifty fellow
  Who had saved up quite a "pile,"
Said he: "I'll buy some presents
  And play Santa Claus awhile."

He chuckled to himself and murmured
  "What a happy thought,"
Then straightaway went into a store
  And here is what he bought:
Some scab-made shirts and neckties
  And a sweatshop suit of clothes,
A pair of shoes made in the "pen";
  Six pairs of scab-made hose.

---

1. Yiddish slang for money.

He planked his union dollars
   On the counter good and hard;
The clerk who took his cash
   Had never seen a Union card.
At the meetings he could boast
   The Union Label with his jaws
But forgot his union principles
   While playing Santa Claus.

From The Machinist Monthly Journal, *December 1937.*

United Brotherhood of Carpenters
and Joiners of America

Though carpenters had tried to form brotherhoods and protective associations since the colonial period, only in 1881 did they succeed in forming a stable, national union. For twenty years, that union stood at the vanguard of labor reform, including the fight for the eight-hour day in the 1880s and 1890s. By 1901, however, the union turned increasingly conservative (comparatively speaking) and evolved into one of the leading proponents of the AFL's business unionism, which preferred collective bargaining to mass strikes and eschewed more radical political movements like Socialism. In the mid-1930s, the union bitterly opposed the Congress of Industrial Organization, and its president, William L. Hutcheson, was the target of John L. Lewis's infamous jab at the 1935 AFL convention in Atlantic City, which many labor historians use to date the split within the labor movement and the subsequent birth of the CIO.

The United Brotherhood of Carpenters frequently printed poems in its monthly journal, though the majority of those poems offered what we would now consider rather bland platitudes about friendship, motherhood, the work ethic, optimism, or the power of a smile. While sharing those impulses, the poems reprinted below offer something else. "Labor," as its title suggests, shows the reverence for labor that inspired even this conservative union, while "From an Old-Timer" offers a poignant and humorous account of life at the Carpenters' own retirement home.

Labor

Bud McKillups

I've builded your ships and your railroads,
I've worked in your factories and mines.
I've builded the roads you ride on.
I've crushed the wild grapes for your wines.

I've worked late at night on your garments.
I've gathered the grain for your bread.
I've builded the house that you live in.
I've printed the books that you've read.

I've linked the two great oceans together.
I've spanned your rivers with steel.
I've builded your towering skyscrapers.
And also your automobile.

I've gone out to wrecked ships in the life-boats.
When the storm loudly cried for its prey.
I've guarded your home from the marauders.
I've turned the night into day.

Wherever there's progress you'll find me.
Without me the world could not live.
And yet you would seek to destroy me,
With the meager pittance you give.

Today you may grind me in slavery.
You may dictate to me from the throne:
But tomorrow I throw off my fetters,
And am ready to claim what I own.

I am master of field and of factory.
I am mighty and you are but few.
No longer I'll bow in submission.
I am LABOR and ask for my due.

From The Carpenter, *April 1930.*

From an Old-Timer

C. Lender

Sykes, old boy, I am feeling so good,
I thought I would write you a letter, at least see if I could:
And tell you something of the gang that is here.[1]
Now please don't get excited for you know that I am queer.
We have some that are blind, and some that are lame,
But most the bunch are still pretty game.
Every once in a while, you would laugh at the sight
Of two of the old boys trying to fight
With one foot in the grave and the other in grease
One would think they'd be trying to live here in peace.
There are English and German, and also Swedes,
Frenchmen and natives, as thick as weeds.
We have them here from most every State,
All busy doing nothing, both early and late.
Some don't like the way his mate wears his hat;
So they keep things popping from this to that.
Some so religious they will most throw a fit
If a fellow gets mad and then cusses a bit.
Some of the old geezers try to play rogue.
They stumble and knock, till their backs nearly broke.
Some wander around as though they were lost;
They can't seem to get used to not being bossed.
Every once in awhile comes a brand new arrival—
Now never mind think such things trivial,
For it takes a whole lot to feed the old things—
You should see this gang hustle when the dinner bell rings.
There are some of them here, perhaps six or seven,
Who would not be contented if they were in heaven.
And some—their names I'll not tell,

---

1. In 1923, the Carpenters Union bought seventeen hundred acres of land near Lake Gibson, Florida, and in 1927 opened a striking Mediterranean-style retirement home. Carpenters who were at least sixty-five years old and had belonged to their union for more than thirty years were guaranteed a small room, food, and a burial plot in a nearby cemetery. At its peak, the home maintained roughly 370 members. It closed in 1976.

Who are in danger of going to!!!
But now let me give you this as a hunch:
Take them all in all, they are not a bad bunch.
But a man who has had so much toil and strife
Had ought to be glad to be living this life.
Now to all the boys in three-thirty-one:
Keep your dues paid ahead, as Lender has done.
Stick fast to your Union—don't quit in a rage,
And you can come here in your old age.
Now Sykes, you might try to write if you can spare the time,
And never mind trying to make it rhyme.

                    Yours till the Bell rings,

                              —Old Man Lender

From The Carpenter, *April 1931. The poem was accompanied by the following note from the editor: "C. Lender, charter member of Local Union No. 331, Norfolk, Va., and at the Carpenters' Home in Lakeland, Fla., sent the following letter home to Brother Sykes."*

United Textile Workers of America

Of all workers during the 1930s, perhaps none suffered as much from the onset of the Great Depression as the hundreds of thousands employed in the textile industry. Many workers were left unemployed or underemployed. Many earned so little in wages that even those with jobs lived in poverty or in decaying company-owned houses. In order to decrease labor costs, even those workers who kept their jobs were assigned to more and more looms, "stretching" them out until the pace of work became almost unbearable. On September 1, 1934, workers revolted, and the United Textile Workers of America led the largest national strike in American history as nearly four hundred thousand textile workers closed mills all along the Atlantic coast. The mill owners, however, fought back, evicting strikers from company houses and enlisting sympathetic state governors to call out the National Guard, which kept the mills open and conducted terror campaigns against striking workers. After several weeks, the strike was called off, some fifteen thousand striking workers were blacklisted, and textile unionism would be a dead letter until the onset of World War II.

The 1934 strike inspired easily the most unusual poet in this collection, Mr. Modestus. Modestus published poems in *The Musician* and in the IWW's newspaper, *Industrial Solidarity,* as well as in *Justice,* the newspaper of the International Ladies Garment Workers Union, but the bulk of his work appeared in *The Textile Labor Banner.* Moreover, his seemingly firsthand knowledge of textile production suggests he either worked or organized in the industry. Regardless of where he worked or published, though, Modestus favored long, at times desultory poems that yoked seemingly disparate subjects into sometimes quite profound statements about life and work during the Depression. The three poems that follow do not break with this pattern. In "Why, oh why?" Modestus compares well-to-do explorers and adventure-seekers with poor, rural folk who move to mill towns and, under the discipline of the factory, eventually express their own desire for adventure by striking. "Fibres" also explores how the textile industry affects workers, placing them at the center of a global industry and ultimately questioning the value of the whole enterprise. Both poems appeared just months after the disappointing conclusion to the 1934 general strike. "'Trust in the Profit System!'" which appeared shortly after those two poems, is a sustained, unqualified indictment of capitalism. In it, Modestus shows that those who lose their religious faith are at risk of blindly putting their faith in the profit system—a faith that will not be rewarded but exploited.

Why, oh why?

Modestus

Why, oh why?
Of course it is just our curiosity
Do comfortable people—
Leave good hotels and modern cooking
The morning papers and the culture of night clubs
And go off
Not half-cocked, but deliberately
Taking passage in funny little steamers
Landing on far off and dangerous beaches
Cumbered with queer commodities—
Leaving paved highways and comfortable conveyance—
For unknown trails to be hacked through unhealthy jungles—
Crawling and sleeping uncertainly—
Among insect-ridden and serpent-studded swamps?

Is it just to get some photographs of wild animals at play?
Or are the pictures an alibi for something else?
Is the body of any such folks too comfortable in the big hotel?
Are their palates soon fed up with the too dainty food?
Is the menace of sudden death in a crowded traffic—
Real enough to us—statistically at least—

Is it too tame a thing to stir their pulses?
Are their eyes hunting to find the looping snakes—
The creeping crocodiles sliding down slimy banks—
Do their ears hark to catch the eerie silence of forest night—
Shattered and heaved by howling hyena choruses—
Or embroidered in pale dawns by twitters of birds and monkeys?
Do their hands itch for the tie-ropes and the slashing knife?
What are the visions which deny peace to their haunted minds?
And—do all these hardy-minded folks go to far-off lands?

Ah, no!
There are other visions of desire—
Haunting the minds of folks who should be content.
Here come the young men, with companions,
Bred in log shacks, back on mountain-spurs,
Learned in gathering their food with rifles,
Or coaxing reluctant corn rows in creek bottoms,
Crowded out of acres which cannot spread wider—
Answering the hum and clang of spinning-mill and loom.
Snug now in two-room cottages—
Near movie-theatre and store—
With dresses gay for girls, and brilliant ties for boys—
They are on the edge of the great world—
Which rises from machines.

Such folk bring with them their sense of far horizons—
It is not long—
Until the slipping threads and inexorable run of cloth—
Which seemed at first the stream on which there flowed to them—
Great, new, and glorious opportunity—
Are changed into a spider's web of circumstance—
That shuts off paths to real release.
The overseer tells them they are right well off—
With white meat, grits, and sugar every week.
Contented ones among them say, it is so.
But visions—from old seeds sprouted in old hills—
Urges inherited from long lines of blood—
Some unexpected consciousness of power—
Drilled and half-disciplined by white mill-whistle blasts—

Unisoned in thought by snapping bobbins—
Wheeled into line by whirling shaft and pulleys—
Agree now in their minds, because their hands—
Have long since learned inevitably—
To release the hidden forces of united action.

New life, and more of life—
New use of powers never known before—
New self-control, which brings controls out-reaching—
New worlds of thought—
New promises of hope that beckon on and upward—
New hills to climb, along the ranges of man's history.
These are the visions haunting brain and soul
When, corn and bacon gained, some room is given—
For generation of impulses long submerged.

The long, straight lines of streets in the mill village—
Grow narrow—end too soon—have no goal.
Perspectives haunt them—beyond the low mill walls—
They will use their powers new born—
Challenge the forces which made them what they are!
Then comes the strike!

From The Textile Labor Banner, *December 10, 1934.*

Fibres

Modestus

Fibres—
Cotton, wool, silk—
Wooden fibres transformed into rayon—
Making up the comforts, ornaments, and decencies—
Of civilizations ancient and modern.
Fibres—
Grown on plants, on worms, on sheep.
Fibres—carded, spun, twisted and woven—

To make garments for dainty women—
Or whirling as belts in machines power-driven
Textiles—
Ginned, washed, scoured, dissolved, extruded—
Carded into yarn,
Spun into threads—
Woven in warp and weft to make textile products.

Textiles—
Multiplied by dollars—
Tangled up in annual dividends—
Made by the fingers of men and women—
In back-grounds of hideous mill-villages—
Amid thousands of bobbins which whirl and hum—
Where looms automatic make clatter and clang—
Weaving fibres in fabrics, sleazy or beautiful—
Weaving heart-throbs, lost hopes, shattered nerves—
Stretching out hands, limbs and eyes—
Over scores of machines—
While weaving a new human pattern—
The union of workers with wills intertwined.

Are they worth what they cost?
These fabrics of beauty, with color and sheen—
Protections from weather—
Keeping us clean and presentable?
The price of their making—
Paid by men, women and children—
Submerged and forgotten—
Compelled to compete in world-markets—
With girls of Japan, or with coolies of China—
Or rag-heads of India—lost in their hills.
What profits a traffic making brutes out of foremen—
Grinding gains from the breaking of children's young backs—
Driving family life into poverty's cesspools—
Whose toiling millions scattered over half a continent—
Hold up business forever sick!

If the gods have decreed that only by such pains—
By wrenching of characters to get such small gains—
If inventions perfected lead only to torture—
While chemistry's marvels are captured by greed—
If cutting of prices for yarn and for cloth—
Means more bitter bargains for live flesh and blood—
If power-plant dams across streams from the hills—
Must mutter the curses of mill-town ills—
It were better to banish all textiles,
Of cloth, yarn, or thread—
And walk in cellophane!

From The Textile Labor Banner, *December 17, 1934.*

"Trust in the Profit System!"

Modestus

"Trust in the Profit System!"
That is the slogan of the managers of industry.
You 18 millions on the FERA relief lists[1]—
Trust in the Profit System!
You 300,000 young folks—
Who have never been able to get a job—
Trust in the Profit System!
You five million heads of families—
Over 45 years old—
Experienced in industry and commerce—
Who are outside the pale of profitable exploitation—
Trust in the Profit System!
You men whose trades have been wiped out by machines—
Whose tools have become useless relics of bygone days—
Whose skill is a forgotten habit—
Whose competence and reliability is unmarketable—

---

1. The Federal Emergency Relief Act, adopted May 1933, provided states with funds for immediate relief—food, clothing, housing—of the unemployed.

Trust in the Profit System!
You mothers—wondering about the future of your babies—
You fathers—seeing the rooftree dissolving over the family home—
Trust in the Profit System!
You holders of certificates of stock—
Useful only for papering walls—
Trust in the Profit System!

If you have lost all faith in Divine Providence—
And are not sure of whether or not—
The ravens will have enough left over to feed you—[2]
Trust in the Profit System!
If you have finished your college course—
Have now finished your engineering training—
Are looking for a place to use this endowment—
Trust in the Profit System!
If your little business has been swallowed up—
Engulfed in a "chain"—
Rubbed out by some eddying circumstance of manufacture—
Fall on your knees—
Lift your heart in confidence—
Look up to the new gods of the world and its markets—
Trust in the Profit System!

The high priests of this cult are preaching in the market places—
They are chanting their rituals in all the courts—
In the places of labor and production—
To the farmers and gardeners and herdsmen—
Their call comes down the wind—
Trust in the Profit System!
But who is this Profit System?
What is behind this call to have blind faith?
What function have those who summon us to a study of this doctrine?
They are the Keepers of the Keys of the Treasure Chests—
In the Temple of Mammon!

From The Textile Labor Banner, *February 9, 1935.*

---

2. Modestus is alluding to 1 Kings 17:4: "And it shall be, that thou shalt drink of the brook; and I have commanded the ravens to feed thee there."

PART II
Unaffiliated Unions

Industrial Workers of the World

From its beginnings at a 1905 convention in Chicago, the Industrial Workers of the World hoped to offer a radical alternative to the election-oriented Socialist Party and, even more so, to the conservative craft unionism of Samuel Gompers and the American Federation of Labor. Unlike the AFL, which organized workers according to their skill or craft (carpenter, painter, machinist), the IWW (like the CIO after it) set out to organize workers by the industry where they worked (railroad, timber, textiles). By doing so, the union hoped to bridge the divisions between and among skilled and unskilled workers, which led to what they jokingly called the American "Separation" of Labor. But perhaps more importantly, the IWW hoped to organize the unorganized: the millions of nominally unskilled immigrant, migrant, and unemployed workers whom the AFL excluded from its craft unions. The IWW also hoped to offer a revolutionary alternative to the AFL, which practiced a sort of "business unionism," meaning they preferred collective bargaining with employers to mass strikes, limited their demands to wages and working conditions, and for the most part accepted the prevailing economic and political order. The IWW, in contrast, sought nothing less than a complete social, political, and above all economic revolution. The preamble to their constitution famously began, "The working class and the employing class have nothing in common," and it followed from that premise that instead of bargaining with employers, workers should practice industrial solidarity, join "one big union," and through militant direct action and the general strike wrestle control over the means of production and distribution from that employing class.

As a "bread and butter" union, however, the IWW had mixed results. Prior to World War I, it led stunning—though mostly failed—strikes among textile workers in Lawrence Massachusetts; silk workers in Paterson, New Jersey; migrant farmworkers throughout the Midwest; and lumber workers in the Pacific Northwest. As a social movement, however, the Wobblies—as they called themselves—had an influence far out of proportion to their inconsistent strike record. They led free speech fights to protect the right to organize, opposed U.S. entry into World War I, and inspired one of the liveliest traditions of working-class culture in American labor history. Songs, poems, and cartoons satirized the employing class, Christian hypocrisy, and the "Mr. Blocks" among the working class who repeatedly failed to recognize the truth—despite costly lessons—about the AFL, employers, and the one big union.

In 1917, however, shortly after the United States entered World War I, the government conducted a national purge of the IWW. In a period of weeks, offices and homes were raided in cities across the country, and thousands of IWW members arrested. Most were imprisoned, including every member of the IWW's executive board. The union never fully recovered.

Despite this repression, though, and despite the rise of other, competing radical political and labor movements in the 1920s and 1930s, the Industrial Workers of the World continued to recruit members and to publish its newspaper, *Industrial Solidarity*. Moreover, many of the poets that had helped make the IWW's reputation—Covington Hall, T-Bone Slim, Ralph Chaplin, and Robert Whitaker—continued to publish new work throughout those decades. In addition to these Wobbly laureates, the IWW attracted many new poets, like the pseudonymous Left Rudder, whose work would also appear in other labor journals throughout the 1930s.

Grin, Clown, Grin

Lola Nolan

When everything in life goes wrong,
And in your heart you find no song,
When you lose your job and your money goes,
And the rent is due, but no one knows
Where it's coming from or how,
Or where the friends are you had till now,
Don't worry, my friend, or grieve yourself thin,
The only sensible thing to do
Is grin.[1]

When day after day things go the same,
And in looking for work you walk yourself lame,
When your shoes get thin, and your coat at the seams
Just holds by a thread, and it almost seems,
Life is a game you are bound to lose—
For the cards are stacked and you cannot choose—
Do not despair, it is only Fate's whim,
The only thing to do, my friend,
Is grin.

Grin when you're hungry, grin when you're cold,
Grin when they tell you you're getting too old,
Grin when you eat your crust of bread.
Grin when you lie down on your hard, cold bed,
Life is simple if you know this rule—
Grin, Clown, Grin—if you're really a fool.

From Industrial Worker, *November 2, 1929.*

---

1. "Grin, Clown, Grin" perhaps cuts even more sharply when read in the context of some of the poems published by more conservative AFL unions, many of which extolled the virtues of "a smile" when confronted with hardship. Here, for example, is the opening stanza of "A Little Smiling," published in the January 1937 edition of *The Carpenter,* the newspaper of the United Brotherhood of Carpenters and Joiners: "Try a little smiling / When the world goes wrong! / Drop that tone of scolding, / Change to one of song; / Nothing lasts forever, / Love and beauty die, / Make the best of the present / Ere it passes by."

Confessions

Covington Ami

I admit it—
I prefer—
Lucifer to Jehovah—

Astarte to Minerva—[1]
Widows to Virgins—
Sinners to Saints—
Reds to Respectables—
Hoboes to Heroes—
"Niggers" to "Supreme Whites"—
And—
Rattlesnakes to Reformers—
The first are All so Much More Interesting—
Put so much more Pep into life—
And—
While they are at it—
Don't care a damn—
Whether or Not—
"Business as Usual"—
Goes to hellornot.—
Same here.

I admit it—
I Don't admire—
He-Men—
She-Women—
Soul-Kissers—
"Captains of Industry"—
"Labor Leaders"—
"Wizards of Finance"—
Dime Distributors—

---

1. Astarte was the Phoenician goddess of fertility and reproduction; the Old Testament condemns her worship because it included sexual and sacrificial rituals. Minerva was the Roman goddess of wisdom, medicine, the arts, science, trade, and war. As in his other comparisons, Hall here confesses his preference for "outcasts" over the officially respectable.

Patriots—
Pollywogs—
And—
Progressifs—
They give me a pain—
They are All so Dull and Dumb—
Damn Respectability, anyhow.

From The Industrial Worker, *December 28, 1929. Covington Ami was one of several pen names—including Covami—Covington Hall adopted. Loosely translated, it means Friend Covington. For more information on Hall, see David Roediger's edited collection of his work,* Labor Struggles in the Deep South *(1999).*

The Skid Road

Anonymous

Dirty sidewalks.
Dirtier streets
Dingy buildings
Smudgy blackboards
Grimy windows
No jobs
Idle workmen
Hands a sleep in empty pockets
Deep set eyes with hungry stares
Dirty pools of water—
Dirt everywhere!
Soft drink joints dispensing stop;
Jangling electric pianos,
Jangling street-cars;
Foul, stale, tobacco-scented card-rooms;
Cheap sensational movies,
Cheap lodging houses
Bootaleggers and de horns!
Pairs and groups of three and four arguing, urging, never agreeing.
Cops, dicks, stoolpigeons.

The home of the cripple, the blind and unfit.
And working men—all greased on skids and going deeper.
It is well named "The Skidroad."[1]

From Industrial Worker, *November 1, 1930.*

---

1. *Skid row* has entered our vocabulary as a general term used to describe a usually run-down section of a city frequented by indigent alcoholics, vagrants, derelicts, and prostitutes, but its precursor, *skid road,* refers to the trail loggers built to slide felled trees down to lumber mills, a practice that developed in the nineteenth-century logging towns of the Pacific Northwest. Loggers would also "grease the skids" with oil to help the trees move more quickly, which the author of "The Skid Road" adopts as a metaphor to describe the declining fortunes of workers.

Nix

William Patton

"Join the Navy! See the tropics! Bask in Cuba's sunny clime!
Join the service with a future, where you have a jolly time.
See the beach at Honolulu and the temples of Siam—
It's a daily round of pleasure when you work for Uncle Sam.
All the clothes are furnished gratis and you never have a care
As you ramble over the ocean blue and Uncle pays the fare;
Where you always eat three times a day and have a place to sleep,
And never seek a box-car when the shades of evening creep;
Where the job is always steady and the pay-day's sure to come."
That's the Navy poster's message to a worker on the bum.

Not a single word is mentioned of the daily grind and plod—
That enlisted men are animals and the officer is God.
It does not tell of hash and beans and eggs of vintage rare—
How forty men together sleep and breathe the unclean air.
There's nothing said of fire-rooms hot; of holystones[1] and paint;
Or how you're put in irons if you dare to make complaint.

---

1. A large, flat piece of sandstone used for scouring a ship's wooden deck.

There's naught of Portsmouth prison[2] with its walls so grim and grey
Where men who show a little guts are sent for years to stay.
It hasn't got a thing to say of life behind the scenes
Such as poison gas and cannon balls, grenades and submarines.

L'envoi

Now though I may make back-door calls and labor for my chuck,
I can always drop the axe or saw and down the alley duck;
So, after much reflection, though it's true I may be dumb,
I think I'll choose the box-car, pal, and stay right on the bum.

From Industrial Worker, *April 18, 1931.*

---

2. Considered the "Alcatraz of the East," Portsmouth Prison was a massive, concrete, castle-like naval prison on Seavey Island in Kittery, off the coast of Maine. It was built between 1905 and 1908 and closed in 1974.

Turning the Corner (The Romantic Quest of Lost Love)

T-Bone Slim

Once again my surging spirit rushes through the eerie murk
And I'd love to gently fondle seven kinds of honest work;
Once again my nature tells me that some labor I should steal
Just to revel in its glory and to glory in its feel.
Oh, I'd love to hold it in my hands, my arms around it clasp;
And I'd squeeze it in my fingers till I made the poor thing gasp;
I would draw it ever closer, coax me sustenance thereof—
Am I growing batty? Nossir—It is simply burning love!

There's a cause for sullen sorrow, for the teardrop in my eye—
For the charms of daily labor is what money cannot buy;
It is something I can't borrow or establish with a sob
And I fear I'll have to essay forth and bungle me a job.
How I used to love my labor, watch it make the kettle boil,
Even as I loved my neighbor, I did love my daily toil;
Even when the selfsame labor had me down to skin and bone—
Please excuse my blind devotion; I feel dreadful, all alone.

Came a day my labor left me, proved unfaithful to her troth,
Left me for to perish, dammit!, or survive the mission broth—
I've survived, but, oh, my brethren, look at what a fearful cost!
Count my ribs and count the poundage my old noble frame has lost.
But I hear my lovely labor, wasted, thin and deadly pale,
Wanders o'er the hills and valleys of this lachrymosal vale,
So I gird my loins a notch or two and leave my cozy shack,
Grab a string of empty box-cars on my lost beloved's track.

Woe is me! the lovely labor hath at last laid down to rest
And, no doubt, she murmured bravely, "I'll have done my very best—"
Nevermore to even snore she tore through miles of sodden dream
And, poor fool, that's me, stood vigil—please excuse me if I scream.
Is it, then, a six-day wonder that my soulful eyes shall blur
When the lovely, lissome labor doesn't lift a leg or stir?
I am lost! but all's forgiven, and my skeleton's good as wired—
When I lifted up the burlap, I found labor had expired.

From Industrial Worker, *August 8, 1931. Born Matti Valentine Huhta (1890?–1942?) in Ashtabula, Ohio, T-Bone Slim was one of the IWW's most famous poets, songwriters, hobos, and activists. He is perhaps best known for his song "The Popular Wobbly."*

Harlan

Ralph Chaplin

Good God! Must I now meekly bend my head
And cringe back to that gloom I know so well?
Forget the wrongs my tongue may never tell,
Forget the plea they silenced with their lead,
Forget the hillside strewn with murdered dead
Where once they drove me—mocked me when I fell—
All black and bloody by their holes of hell,
While all my loved ones wept uncomforted?[1]

---

1. Beginning in 1931, miners in Harlan, Kentucky, some facing starvation from lack of work, rebelled against the layoffs, wage reductions, and the practice of being paid in devalued company scrip that then characterized most Appalachian coal mines. The owners of the coal

Is this the land my fathers fought to own—
Here where they curse me, beaten and alone?
But God, it's cold! My children sob and cry!
Shall I go back into the mines and wait,
And lash the conflagration of my hate—
Or shall I stand and fight them till I die?

From Industrial Worker, *February 9; 1932. Ralph Chaplin (1887–1961) was one of the IWW's most revered poets, organizers, and editors. Born in Kansas, raised in Chicago, Chaplin became a socialist while still a teenager, traveled to Mexico, and then returned to Chicago, where he worked as a commercial artist and itinerant labor organizer. He joined the IWW in 1913 and shortly thereafter became editor of its newspaper,* Solidarity. *Arrested during the government's purge of the IWW in 1917, Chaplin served four years in prison and then returned to the labor movement. He is perhaps best known today for penning the lyrics to "Solidarity Forever," the unofficial anthem of the labor movement. He published an autobiography,* Wobbly: Rough and Tumble Story of an American Radical, *in 1948.*

---

mines, however, struck back, viciously, making "Bloody Harlan" one of the most violent moments in American labor history. By mid-1931, the local sheriff, at the behest of the mine owners, had deputized sixty-five hired thugs who raided miners' homes, periodically attacked them, and as a group murdered at least eleven striking mine workers. On the eve of a January 1, 1932, strike, which Chaplin's poem indirectly refers to, two Harlan County miners were murdered, and shortly thereafter, the miners' union headquarters were raided, effectively ending the strike.

The Sin of Hoarding

William E. Patton

We thought that the workers were hungry
Because they were unemployed,
But when Hoover accused them of hoarding[1]
Such thoughts were quite quickly destroyed;

---

1. As part of his 1932 reelection campaign, President Herbert Hoover blamed the Great Depression on what he described as the wide-scale hoarding of currency. In a March 1932 radio address, Hoover told America, "I believe that the individual American has not realized the harm he has done when he hoards even a single dollar away from circulation" and that "no one will deny that if the vast sums of money hoarded in the country today could be brought into active circulation there would be a great lift to the whole of our economic progress."

The guy who picks bits from the garbage
So the wife and the kids can be fed
Is doing it just cause he's stingy
And won't spend a nickel for bread.

The fellow who sleeps in the alley
With his head on a pillow of rock
Is merely a chiseling cheapskate
With plenty dough in his sock.

There are some who are ragged and tattered
With shoes that are worn off their feet—
They've got dough sewn up in a mattress,
But the mattress is out in the street.

When you see people feeble and sickly
With complexion as pallid as snow,
They're hoarding their cash from the doctor—
To the morgue they'd much rather go.

When the sheriff moves all your belongings
To the sidewalk for not paying rent,
You're just having fun with the landlord,
You could pay him his dough to a cent.

When your overcoat lays in a pawnshop
And you've peddled the old family clock,
You're a miserly two-timing hoarder,
Too stingy to dig in your sock.

But don't blame the boss for your troubles
As he rides in his Chrysler or Stutz
Though he smokes good cigars, he's a spender—
It's you who are hoarding the butts.

From Industrial Worker, *April 8, 1932.*

Heat Portraits

310 Bulletin

This is Boulder City,[1] all smothered in heat,
Gunmen and lizards, roaming the street,
Bull pen at one end, Butcher Heights at the other
Hey, fellow worker, did you ever see a prison?

Into the poolroom with all his hardware
He sticks out here, and he sticks out there,
He is the chief, you should know that—
Say, have you been to Midway lately?

Yep that's it, once chased boes on the great U.P.,[2]
Now it rides herd on you and me,
Take a look from its eyes to the top of its head—
What's a moron fellow worker?

Pistol Pete coming down the street
Swinging his arms and throwing his feet,
A fake on his hip, a twist to his walk,—
Did you ever hop clods behind a mule-drawn cotton plow?

Up the street to the legion hall,
Something on a scaffold, smearing paint on the wall,
It wiggles its ears and shakes its head—
Have you ever heard how the butcher made the pigshead nonunion?

From Industrial Worker, *August 23, 1932.*

---

1. Boulder City, Nevada, near the Colorado River, was initially created by the federal government to house the thousands of workers who helped build Hoover Dam. By 1935, over five thousand workers were employed on the project, with many thousands more arriving in Boulder City and nearby Las Vegas in search of work. Those who did manage to find work on the dam labored under almost unimaginable conditions. In the summer, temperatures routinely rose to 140 degrees and, officially at least, 112 workers died during construction, though that number is almost certainly too low. The IWW led two strikes at the dam, one in August 1931 and another in August 1932, both of which failed, and during which many union activists were arrested—hence this anonymous poet's surrealist focus on not just the heat but also the jails and the police of Boulder City.
2. Union Pacific, the (notoriously antiunion) railroad line; "boes" are hoboes.

The Migratory I.W.W.

Jack Kenney

He's one of the fellows that doesn't fit in;
You have met him without a doubt.
He's lost to his friends, his kith and his kin
As he tramps the world about.

At night he wanders beneath the stars,
With the mien of an ancient seer,
And often he's humming a few sweet bars
Of a rebel song soft and clear.

Yes, he's one of the breed that never fits
And never a dollar can glean.
He's one that a scornful world requites
As simply a might-have-been.

But deep in the heart of his hungry soul
Though the smug world casts him out,
There burns like the flames of a glowing coal
The fire of a love devout.

For a better world in which men may live
With plenty for one and all,
Where no slave shall bow to a boss's greed,
Nor answer a parasite call.

From Industrial Worker, *May 1, 1934.*

Hell

Harold Allinger

A shepherd froze on the desert,
A logger drowned in the drive,
A train crew killed in a R.R. wreck,
A miner buried alive;
The annual death toll of labor
No-one will ever tell;
Some say "industrial hazard"
But the workers call it "Hell."

Jealousy over a market,
A quarrel over a debt,
Armies moving to action
And war's grim stage is set,
Workers slaying their fellows
With gas, bullet and shell;
Some may call it "PATRIOTISM"
But the victims call it "Hell."

Many wondrous devices,
To do the work of men,
To ease their irksome burdens
And make them free again;
But ever the pace grows faster
And master's profits swell;
Some call it "Machine production,"
But the workers call it "Hell."

Toilers retaining only,
Enough to live and breed,
Leeches hoard and devour
Untold wealth in their greed;
Crime, War and Perversion
Starvation and prison cell;
Some call it "Civilization,"
But the proper name is "Hell."

From Industrial Worker, *October 1934.*

The Shape Up

Left Rudder

Of all the sights that I have seen
On waterfronts where I have been—
And I can boast of vision keen—
The weirdest was a "Shape-Up" scene.[1]

To think that images of God,
For food, for shelter, and for shod
Should willingly to "shape-up" plod,
To say the least, is strange and odd.

With buttons on their hats and lapes,
They all form up in half moon shapes
With faces garbed in hopeful drapes
While each man on the straw boss gapes.

This question then in rhyming scrawl
I'd like to ask you, one and all,
Tony, Pat and John and Paul
And other names I can't recall—
Why handle freight, and wheel, and haul,
Like felons bound with chain and ball
For such job crumbs as choose to fall
When hours are long and pay is small,
When instead you could install
A hiring system fair to all,
Rotating from your Union Hall?

Why stand in "Shape Up" like a thrall
Or scramble, push and rush and brawl,
Or, to the Straw Boss cringe and crawl?

From Industrial Worker, *November 21, 1936.*

---

1. At the morning "shape-up," crowds of unemployed and underemployed longshoremen gathered at seaport docks to compete for the attention of a foreman, who would choose a fraction of the men for a day's work moving and stowing ship cargoes. Dockworkers resented the chaos, favoritism, degradation, low wages, and jealousy that the shape up produced, and in the 1934 San Francisco general strike they sought to control the hiring process through the union hall, where a limited pool of workers would be selected on a rotating basis.

Madrid

Robert Whitaker

When I wake up in the night to remembrance
   Of the sorrow and strife of the day,
The perils of people and nations,
   The portents of battle array,
I am cheered despite all of the horror,
   Whatever the hell-makers did,
That the Fascists still fail of their purpose,
   Nor yet have they taken Madrid.[1]

I am stricken with shame that the many
   So easily fall for the fools,
That morons and madmen are quicker
   For union than statesmen and schools.
But though the world's leaders are flabby,
   And spineless as polyps or squid,[2]
The Fascists still fail of their purpose,
   Nor yet have they taken Madrid.

And I know that whatever may happen,
   However appalling the cost;
Though all the defenses are fallen,
   And everything seems to be lost;
The seed of a freer tomorrow
   Beyond all destruction is hid;
And the Fascists shall learn, to their sorrow,
   Not yet have they taken Madrid.

From Industrial Worker, *March 13, 1937.*

---

1. In February 1936, Spain elected a progressive, republican government that promised much-needed reform in national policies affecting education, land, and the economy. In July of that year, the military, led by General Francisco Franco, and with the support of conservative capitalists and the Catholic Church, rebelled against the new government, setting off a lengthy and deadly civil war that attracted the sympathies and sacrifices of people worldwide. Madrid, the capital of Spain, remained in Republican control until the very conclusion of the war, despite repeated efforts by the Fascists to take the city. As Whitaker's poem suggests, to its defenders and sympathizers Madrid represented more than just the city; its survival, whether in reality or in memory, symbolized the continued survival of democracy, freedom, and workers' rights themselves.
2. With the exception of the Soviet Union, the major Western powers—France, Britain, and the United States—refused to provide aid to Spain in its fight against Franco and Fascism.

The Line-Up

John G. Hirschfeldt

Stand in line and state your grief,
Stand in line if you want relief,
Stand in line to get some chuck,
Stand in line to take a truck
to take you to a camp
Where they treat you like a tramp.[1]

Stand in line to check your trunk,
Stand in line to get your bunk,
Stand in line to get deloused,
Stand in line to get housed.
In double-decked barracks, like convicts of yore,
Where in seven different keys they snore.

Stand in line to get your eats,
Stand in line to get your sheets.
Stand in line on tobacco day—
For that is the only pay the state gives
You for thirty hours work a week,
So be gentle and nice and meek.

This is what California's done
To Roosevelt's forgotten men.[2]
To change all this, my friends, get wise—
Stand in line and organize.

From Industrial Worker, *Sept. 17, 1938.*

---

1. Driven by the Great Depression, drought, dust storms, and the mechanization of farm labor, thousands of farmers and their families migrated to California with the hope of finding work. In response to this influx of workers, the State of California set up labor camps, many of which represented an improvement over the poor sanitation and public health problems of the migrants' own camps; these state-run camps, however, sometimes resembled prisons and forced-labor camps more than relief programs.
2. Although Franklin Roosevelt frequently invoked this phrase, "the forgotten man," in his speeches and rhetoric, it first appears in an April 7, 1932 radio address titled "The Forgotten Man." "These unhappy times call for the building of plans that rest upon the forgotten, the unorganized but the indispensable units of economic power, for plans like those of 1917 that build from the bottom up and not from the top down, that put their faith once more in the forgotten man at the bottom of the economic pyramid."

Surpluses, O the Surpluses!

Covington Hall

The surpluses! The surpluses! They're choking us to death![1]
There's so much air around us we can hardly get a breath!
There's so much silk and cotton, rayon, ramie, linen, wool,
The children must wear overalls or stay away from school.

The surpluses! The surpluses! All industries they stall!
There's so awful much of plenty that a famine threatens all!
There's so much milk and bread and butter, wine and fruit and meat,
There's not enough for everyone to get a filling eat!

The surpluses! The surpluses! 'Tis horrible to ken
What the surpluses are doing to the hordes of surplus men
Who lost their jobs producing what they couldn't purchase back,
Who filled the land with plenty but now hold an empty sack.

The surpluses! The surpluses! They're driving statesmen wild!
They've got our great Economists and all our Brain Trusts riled![2]
They've got them all explaining that our only hope on Earth
Is to end this dread abundance with an artificial dearth!

---

1. Many economists during the 1930s blamed the Great Depression on the presence of "surpluses," the glut of goods that resulted from advances in manufacturing and agricultural productivity in the 1920s. By the 1930s, these economists argued, workers and their families did not earn enough to buy those goods, thus leading to what they called "underconsumption." Moreover, so long as factories and farms retained surpluses, there was no incentive to produce new goods or hire new workers, thus prolonging the Depression. As a result, most of the New Deal economic programs sought to address this stagnation, sometimes by attempting to increase people's ability to purchase goods, but often through deliberately limiting production, especially of agricultural goods. In 1931, for example, in order to drive up demand and prices, the Louisiana state legislature prohibited farmers from planting cotton. By 1933, the Agricultural Adjustment Administration had made these policies national. In the spring of that year, the AAA paid farmers to plow up roughly ten million acres of cotton and to slaughter six million baby pigs. The program made a certain crude economic sense, but destroying crops and food while people went unclothed and unfed struck many as mad and possibly criminal. As one farm leader put it, a sentiment that Hall's poem expresses though with more irony, "That we should have idle and hungry and ill-clad millions on the one hand, and so much food and wool and cotton upon the other that we don't know what to do with it, this is an utterly idiotic situation, and one which makes a laughing stock of our genius of a people."
2. "Brain Trusts" refer to the group of academics, mostly economists, whom Franklin Delano Roosevelt enlisted to advise him during his first years as President.

The surpluses! The surpluses! They're busting rich and poor!
They're making folks lose confidence in all the creeds of yore!
In spite of all our sabotage, in spite of all our wars,
The awful curse of plenty still the Nation's welfare mars!

The surpluses! The surpluses! They're choking us to death!
There's so much air around us we can hardly get a breath!

From Industrial Worker, *July 23, 1938.*

The Curious Christians

Covington Hall

For "Jesus' sake" they shoot you dead,
They fill you full of gas and lead;
They wreck your body, crush your soul,
Then pray to God to "make you whole."

They stand for war,—with fervent breath
They bless the instruments of death;
They cheer the flag, they shout for blood,
They weep beside the crimson flood.

They strike the light from woman's eyes,
They "charitably" hush her cries;
They slay the husband, take her child,
Then tract her on "love undefiled."

They say, "'Tis not by bread alone
That mankind cometh to its own";
Then strive to bind the spirit's wings,
The upward surge of changing things.

They preach "good will" and "peace" and "love,"
"The golden rule," all else above;
They teach Man's brotherhood as true,
Then turn their war-dogs loose on you.

Ah, verily, they say and say,
And preach and preach, and pray and pray;
Yet still the harvest comes as sown,
Still "by its fruit the tree is known."[1]

From Industrial Worker, *December 2, 1939.*

---

1. Although the exact phrase comes from Matthew 12:32–33 ("Either make the tree ideal or its fruit ideal, or make the tree rotten and its fruit rotten, for by its fruit the tree is known"), Hall more likely has in mind Matthew 7:20–21: "Beware of false prophets, which come to you in sheep's clothing, but inwardly they are raving wolves. Ye shall know them by their fruits."

To a Nine-Inch Gun

Anonymous

Whether your shell hits the target or not,
Your cost is five hundred dollars a shot.
Your thing of noise and flame and power,
We feed you a hundred barrels of flour
Each time you roar. Your flame is fed
With twenty thousand loaves of bread.
Silence! A million hungry men
Seek bread to feed their mouths again.

From Industrial Worker, *December 23, 1939.*

To the Spinachers
Albert Brocken X202600.

Slavery days are on again[1]
In spinach fields so fine—

Watsonville[2] is the place,
Eight-thirty is the time.

Sun is shining, weather's great;
Yet, it looks like rain.
But don't worry, boss, we'll hurry;
Please don't raise no cane.

We're all lined up, I've got a crate;
Each man is on a row.
We all sit tense, our sharp knives out,
The bossman yells, "Let's go."

The race is on our knives they flash
As we cut off the spinach—
I can see by the rate the others go
I'll be behind in the finish.

I've been cutting spinach for 'bout an hour;
I look, It's half-past nine.
I roll a smoke and light her up—
Now, to charge that line!

I must give up; It ain't no use,
I cannot win this race.
Their heads are down, their moons are up,
They set too fast a pace.

---

1. May echo the popular song "Happy Days Are Here Again," which was played at the 1932 Democratic presidential convention and which Franklin Roosevelt adopted as a campaign song.
2. Watsonville, California, just south of San Francisco, near the Santa Clara Valley, where many Mexican (and Filipino, Anglo, and occasionally African American) migrant farm laborers conducted a series of bloodily repressed strikes in 1934.

The boss comes 'round and says to me:
"Could you go a little faster?"
I says to him, so honestly,
"This job I'll try to master."

Why work long hours in a spinach field,
Thirty-five cents an hour for pay
When you can increase your pay per hour
And work fewer hours a day?

O slaves on agricultural jobs,
Why don't all of you get wise?
Why don't you beat the bosses to the punch?
Why don't you organize?

Join the Industrial Workers of the World,
One Big Union strong,
Become a class conscious worker—
We know that you won't go wrong.

From Industrial Worker, *December 23, 1939. The series of numbers following Brocken's name is his union membership number, which many IWW members used to identify themselves.*

Sailors Union of the Pacific

From 1895 to 1936, the Sailors Union of the Pacific was the only thriving affiliate of the largely ineffective AFL-affiliated International Seamen's Union, which sought to represent the thousands of sailors on merchant ships who had historically worked under horrific conditions, including poor food, cramped living quarters, and autocratic officers. In 1936, however, the SUP joined the Maritime Federation of the Pacific, an independent association of maritime unions on the West Coast under the leadership of Harry Bridges, and was promptly expelled from the AFL. Its newspaper, *West Coast Sailor,* published numerous poems.

The Company Union

R. F. Steltemeier

The Company formed a Union[1]
  And they met without delay.
And the simpletons concluded
  They were getting too much pay.
So they voted for a reduction
  And the company O.K.'d
Every act of self destruction
  That these silly numbskulls made.

---

1. On company unions, see note to "Company Unionism" under the Brotherhood of Maintenance of Way Employes.

They scoffed about eight hours
　And declared they wanted ten.
The firm told them how proud they were
　To have such loyal men.
Then they passed a resolution
　With a vigorous hurray,
That to please the company they'd live
　On just one meal a day.

From West Coast Sailor, *July 2, 1937.*

The Live One

Anonymous

The birds of prey come swooping down
When his ship comes steaming by.
The reception committee's tremendous—
Holy Christ, what a popular guy.

A bunch of beachcombers are laying in wait
As he leaves midships with his pay;
And a couple of haybags are on the dock
To make sure that he don't get away.

Payday night—and he leans against the bar
And boasts of the feats he has done;
How he socked the skipper on the chin
And put the chief mate on the run.

The bartender listens with bulging eyes
And "yeses" him frequently.
And the barroom bums all nod their heads,
For the drinks are coming free.

The floozies all give him a great big hand;
He's surrounded by blushing brides.
He does not know what attracts them so
Is merely the dough in his "strides."

But next night he's broke and he wanders about
And his "friends" all pass him by.
Yes, his audience of the night before
Now gives him the glassy eye.

The girls who had mobbed him the night before,
Tonight with him are not booked,
For another ship has paid off that day
And a fresh live wire has been hooked.

Well, such is fame, he has had his fun;
Now he'll look for another ship.
He'll stay away from such phoney joints
Till he makes another trip.

L'envoie

You may think this rhyme is all the bunk
And its moral much too strong;
But this is the slogan of the beach:
THE LIVE ONE IS NEVER WRONG!

From West Coast Sailor, *February 23, 1940.*

A Brother's Complaint

Anonymous

Sis is going with a "sailor,"
At first it didn't faze us:
But now the family's talk is full
Of sailor's salty phrases.

We all found it rather hard
To follow all his speech;
For they talk different on-board ship
Than we do "on the beach."

For when the time to eat comes,
He sings out "chow" for food;
And always "stows it down the hatch,"
Which Grandma says is rude.

When talking during dinner,
He talks like other boys;
Except he calls the lettuce "grass,"
And celery just plain "noise."

His salty talk is slangy,
And hard to understand;
He calls canned milk "iron cow,"
And sugar he calls "sand."
His many names for coffee
Are certainly for a joke;
He calls it everything from "mud"
To "Joe" to just plain "Jamoke."

The spinach he calls "Popeye,"
And Grandma always squirms
To hear him ask for spaghetti
And say "throw me the Worms."

The chicken he calls "sea-gull,"
The ketchup is "red-lead"
The waffles are "collision mats,"
While "punk" is mother's bread!

Fried fish is "Pedro's pork chops,"
"Seadust" is his name for salt;
When he called the pepper "fly-specks,"
Ma nearly called a halt.

He sat beside my father,
And needed elbow room,
He looked at Dad and said, "Say Mate,
Rig in your starboard boom."

We finally all caught on tho,
And now we're doing fine;
We say "Six bells" for three o'clock,
When we are telling time;

When Ma goes to the city
Or runs down to the store;
And someone asks us where she is,
We say she's "gone ashore."

Sister calls a floor a "deck,"
To hear her talk is sport;
To her a roof's an "overhead,"
A window is a "port."

Then too if something gets "fouled up,"
Or some new trouble comes,
And Dad starts to complain, Ma says,
"Now Pa, don't beat your gums."

Dad doesn't tie his tie now,
Instead he "bends it on,"
While Grandma says the kids "shoved off,"
Instead of they have gone.

Ma says dad's suit is "shipshape,"
If it is fitting him;
But if it's not so neat she says,
"That lash ain't up so trim."

When Pappy goes to work now,
We say he's "turning to;"
While Mother "swabs," and never scrubs,
As she once used to do.

The whole place has gone salty,
Which makes me lots of trouble;
For when Ma says "Come here, 'chop-chop'"
I go there. . . "on the double."

I wish that sailor would "weigh anchor,"
And do what of I think:
And "point his bow" and "trim his jib,"
And go jump in the "drink."

I'm through "batting the breeze" and
"Singing the blues" I'm sure;
So for the night I'll just "turn in,"
"Cease firing," and "secure."

From West Coast Sailor, *April 5, 1940.*

Southern Tenant Farmers' Union

In July 1934, eighteen black and white sharecroppers in eastern Arkansas started the Southern Tenant Farmers' Union, and just one year later the union could count some ten thousand members throughout the Delta region. At its outset, the STFU hoped to amend some of the inequities of the Agricultural Adjustment Administration, one of the Roosevelt administration's first major recovery programs, but, as their poetry shows, the union did not hesitate to indict the entire system of sharecropping itself.

Under that system, which replaced slavery as the primary mode of agricultural production in the South following the Civil War, sharecroppers would rent farms from large landholding planters, agreeing to pay the landowner a share of the crop—usually half—at the end of the season. In turn, landowners would supply the sharecropper with seed, supplies, and food, deducting the cost of those supplies from the tenant farmer's eventual share. (Farmers who owned their own land entered similar arrangements with "furnishing merchants," purchasing supplies on credit and agreeing to pay back the loan from the subsequent sale of their crops.) Because of the steady decline in cotton prices, however, together with the inflated prices landowners and merchants charged for supplies, sharecroppers and farmers often ended the agricultural season in debt, thus beginning a cycle of poverty, landlessness, and exploitation that could last for generations.

The Great Depression exacerbated these tendencies toward poverty and exploitation, especially as the price of cotton fell even lower. Officials in Roosevelt's administration sought to raise the income of farmers by raising the price of the agricultural goods they sold, which they hoped to accomplish by paying farmers to leave all or some of their land uncultivated, thereby driving up demand. As some of the poetry included in this anthology demonstrates, this program would cause a minor scandal, but it had much more immediate and devastating effects for the sharecroppers themselves. AAA payments went directly to planters and landowners, who, despite a law forbidding such a practice, frequently withheld shares of the payments that rightly belonged to their tenant farmers. Instead of relieving sharecropper poverty, then, in many cases the AAA worsened it. Moreover, as planters began to reduce the amount of land they cultivated, they rented fewer and fewer acres to sharecroppers and soon started evicting them from their farms and houses.

Aided by Norman Thomas, leader of the Socialist Party, the STFU organized among African American and white farmers alike, seeking to improve sharecropper conditions, stop evictions, and secure fair share payments. In August 1935, the STFU led a strike that resulted in a significant increase in the pay rate for harvested cotton, and following widespread evictions in January 1936, the STFU urged evicted sharecroppers to set up tent colonies along highways in order to publicize their misery and planters' indifference, successfully drawing the nation's attention and condemnation. The union had less success winning parity payments from the AAA Cotton Section, however, which throughout the 1930s remained primarily organized for and friendly toward the planters. Throughout it all, and as the STFU grew, planters conducted a semipermanent reign of terror on union leaders and sympathizers, hiring police officers and other citizens to arrest, beat, and, in several cases, murder STFU activists. After a failed attempt at affiliating with the CIO in 1937, by the end of 1939 the STFU closed its doors.

Nevertheless, the union left a remarkable legacy of poets and poems. Early poems, like "Share-Cropper's Choice" and "The Sharecropper," describe the impoverished working and living conditions among sharecroppers; so too, in its way, does "Good Ol' Pete," a dialect poem by the IWW poet and activist Covington Hall, who contributed the poem to the STFU newspaper, *The Sharecroppers' Voice*. Like Sterling Brown's better-known "Slim Greer" sequence, Hall's poem draws on the tradition of African American folk poetry and tall tales, as well as the "heaven and hell" poems ("Casey Jones," for example) that is a staple of earlier union poetry and song. The remaining poems are by John Henry, the pseudonym of the self-described "Negro Poet and Organizer" of the STFU, John Handcox. Handcox's poems, especially "Landlord, What in the Heaven is the Matter with You?" anticipate much of the rhetorical and political militancy of the Black Arts poets of the 1960s.

Share-Cropper's Choice

Anonymous

Up early in the morning,
Only a bite to eat,
Mostly Bread and Molasses
Never a bite of meat.
Plowing long rows of cotton
Till noon bell calls to eat
Bean-soup, bread, and molasses
Never a bite of meat.

Plowing in evening sunshine
Tired, too darned tired to eat
Beans, Corn-bread, and molasses
But it's that _____ or organize.

From The Sharecroppers' Voice, *June 21, 1935.*

The Sharecropper

Anonymous

He grows great fields of cotton
He works long hours each day;
But the way he lives is rotten
Because of such poor pay.

His wife and children help him
To grow clothes for the world;
But the way they dress is shameful
At them insults are hurled.

They're called "no 'count" and "lazy"
And if they dare complain
They're told that they are crazy
And have themselves to blame.

Sharecroppers, join the Union
And all together stand.
No power then can rob you
Of the bounties of the land.

From The Sharecroppers' Voice, *August 1935.*

Good Ol' Pete

Covington Hall

Slufoot Sam en his gal, Lou,
Rode up dar on er kangaroo;
Dey rode up dar, ez sho' as fate,
Straight up dar ter de Pearly Gate;
Dey knock en knock, 'twel 'ol man Pete
Came hurrin' down de Golden Street;
En den dey say: "Am you de Saint,
Is you who says who's in ur aint?"
Pete look at Sam, he look at Lou,
En lakwaz at de kangaroo;
En den he say, "Well! Howdydoo!
Whut kin we all do fo' you?"
Den dis dey 'low: "We's sick uv sin;
We wants ter know kin we git in?
We's done our sheer down dar on Earth;
We's hoed de cotton frum our birth;
We's paid mo' rent en intres', too,
Dan Gawd hissef kin count fo' you;
We's wucked en scraped, en don't know yet
How much we's in de landlord's debt;
We's all wore out, we sho' is Pete;
We'd lak er house on Easy Street."
Den Pete he say, "Dat sho' wuz hell!
Walk right in en res' er spell."

From The Sharecroppers' Voice, *December 1935. The poem was accompanied by the following note from Hall: "The Slufoot Sams are not numbered among the Negroes alone, but also among White, Mexicans, etc."*

The Planter and the Sharecropper

John Henry, Union Organizer, Southern Tenant Farmers' Union

The Planter lives off the sweat of the sharecroppers brow
Just how the sharecropper lives the planter cares not how
The cropper raises all the planter can eat
Then gets tramped down under his feet.
The sharecropper raises all the planter can wear
While he and his family have to go bare
The sharecropper works, toils, and sweats
The Planter brings him out in debt.
The planter has good and wholesome food to eat
The sharecropper has corn bread molasses and Fat back meat
A lot of good things the planters have to waste
The sharecropper don't know how it taste.
The sharecropper's wife goes to washtub, kitchen, and field
While the planter's wife enjoys herself in an automobile
The planters children dress up and go to school
While the sharecroppers children put on rags and follow a mule.
If you ask a planter for your right
You might as well spit in his face and ask for a fight.
The planter says he inherited his wealth by birth
But it all comes from the poor man who tills the earth
The planters get together they plot and they plan
You bet your life it's against the poor man
The planter takes the sharecropper's mule, wagon or plow.
He don't allow them to have a hog or cow.
The planter lives in a house as fine as the best
And wears good clothes and all the rest
Makes no difference how much the sharecropper's raise
The planters get all the Praise.
When the sharecropper dies he is buried in a box
Without a necktie or without any socks
The sharecropper works hard and wears cotton sacks
And lives in raggedy, filthy broken down shacks.
The poor man has fought all the rich man's wars
And now we are punished without any cause

The sharecropper labors the planters pockets to swell
But the planters unjust deeds are sending him straight to Hell.
Now no rich planter to be ever do I crave
But I do want to be something more than a planter's slave
If any one thinks this ain't the truth
He can go through Arkansas and get the proof.

From The Sharecroppers' Voice, *March 1936. "John Henry" is the pseudonym of John Handcox, the poet laureate of the Southern Tenant Farmers' Union. Handcox (1904–92) was born in Brinkley, Arkansas, and was himself a tenant farmer. He joined the STFU in 1935 and became one of its most active organizers, publicists, and fund-raisers. Handcox is better remembered today, though, for his songs and poems. In addition to the three poems Handcox published in* The Sharecroppers' Voice *(included here), he also composed many songs, which he would play at STFU meetings. In 1937, on a trip to Washington, DC, Handcox recorded some of these songs and poems for Charles Seeger (the folk singer Pete Seeger's father), who worked for the Library of Congress. After introducing Woodie Guthrie to Handcox's work, Pete Seeger and Guthrie included some of Handcox's work—including the poem "The Planter and the Sharecropper"—in Alan Lomax's collection* Hard Hitting Songs for Hard Hit People *(1967). One of Handcox's songs, "Roll the Union On," has since become a union anthem, though few remember its origins or author. In the mid-1980s there was renewed interest in Handcox's life and work. He made various appearances commemorating the fiftieth anniversary of the founding of the STFU, and the labor songwriter Joe Glazer and the labor historian Michael Honey interviewed Handcox for the Library of Congress. The West Virginia University Press later issued a CD,* John Handcox: Songs, Poems, and Stories of the Southern Tenant Farmers Union *(2004), which reproduces the original Library of Congress recordings (including Handcox reciting this poem and "Landlord, What in the Heaven is the Matter with You") as well Glazer and Honey's 1985 interview.*

Landlord, What in the Heaven is the Matter with You?

John Henry, Negro Poet and Organizer STFU

Landlord, what is the matter with you?
Just what has labor ever done to you?
Upon their backs you always ride
Don't you think labor ever gets tired?
For many years you have taken all the laborer has made.
You have taken the cotton and all the corn
And left the worker nothing to live upon.
Labor is human and is only asking for right
You are evicting us, beating us and cheating us and wanting to fight

You have treated your labor all so mean
That they have nothing to eat but motherless turnip greens.
I'll tell the world that the labor has nothing to eat
But corn bread and motherless greens without any meat
Landlord what in the Heaven is the matter with you?
The Bible says do unto others as you would have them do unto you.
In 1933 no checks, when we plowed up cotton
Some of that money labor has never gotten
You pledged the government your labor you would pay
But you put it in your pocket and went on your way.
In the AAA Contract nineteen and thirty four
You chiseled your Labor out of some more
In 1935 the parity money your Labor you deprived
In 1936 the substitute AAA you all are trying to fix.
We all hope it will be so that you get yours and no more
Your labor you have always robbed and just because they want their rights
    you want them mobbed.
In the heat and the cold for you your labor went
And in the cold winter you threw them out to live in tents.
You landlords get together and have some black hearted "Nigger" to print a
    paper
It's known as the Southern Liberator which says the man who works gets
    what he wants
That's a stinkin lie "You know he don't"
Further you advise Labor not to buy Baloney, sardines, and cheese
You want them to continue to buy cornbread and peas.
You have taken all your Labors Rights now you want to take his appetite.
You say move away from landlords who are unfair
You must want us to live in the air.
You said landlords like Beck and Twist and such
Pay their money for long term schools
You must think all us workers are fools
Now Landlord just what in the Heaven is the matter with you?
Remember the poor man loves his wife and children too.
When Workers get old or sick then off the land them you kick.
You ride in you cars and have a good time you plan and you figure,
You bet your life it's against poor white man and the nigger

You disfranchise them and wont let them vote
When they have all the load to tote.
Now, Landlord, what is the matter with you?
Labor has never had anything to say as to what you join.
We have never broken up your meeting or your churches burned
From none of your meetings have you, by your labor been hailed
Nor beaten with an ax handle, shot in the back or put in jail.
When you were not honest and wouldn't do right
Labor has never shot in your homes or thrown dynamite
Now Arkansaw would be a fine place to live you bet
If the Saw didn't have such a bad set.
Landlord what in the Heaven is the matter with you?

From The Sharecroppers' Voice, *May 1, 1936. The poem was accompanied by the following note from the editor: "One of the first issues [of* The Southern Liberator, *a rival, planter-backed newspaper] called to our attention called upon the Negro laborer to refuse to act with the white members of the Southern Tenant Farmers Union to secure better conditions and advised that they co-operate with the planters and let the poor white workers struggle alone. The next issue carried a front page editorial, entitled 'Farm Labor What in the Hell is the Matter With You.' This editorial praised the plantation system and states that planters were providing schools and such for Negro Workers. We are giving space to a young Negro Poet, John Henry, to answer this in the current issue of the* Voice, *'Landlord, What in the Heaven is the Matter with You,' don't fail to read it."*

The Union Song

John Henry, Organizer

Have you ever woke up in the morning
And it seemed like your day of toil started wrong?
Nothing in this world would console you
But to start singing the good old union song?

Some time you go to the window or door and begin
Wondering and looking out across the field
Thinking of what wealth the farmers have added to the nation
While they have to live on such scant yield.

Be of good cheer, be patient, be faithful
And help the Union to grow strong
And if at any time you are discouraged
Revive yourself by singing the good old union song.

When thinking of how horrid the past has been
Knowing that labor's road has not been smooth,
Deep down in your heart you keep singing
"We shall not, we shall not be moved."

From The Sharecroppers' Voice, *October–November 1936.*

PART III ————————————————————————————

Congress of Industrial Organizations

International Ladies Garment Workers Union

Until the Civil War, most clothing was made either by skilled tailors and dressmakers or by individuals and their families. By the turn of the twentieth century, however, a number of developments—in manufacturing, in advertising, in the growth of chain stores and mail-order catalogs—led more and more people, especially women, to purchase "ready-made" or "ready-to-wear" clothing manufactured according to predetermined sizes. As a result of this shift in the manufacture and consumption of clothing, the garment industry turned into one of the most profitable—if also competitive, volatile, and exploitative—industries in the country.

Located predominantly in and around New York City, garment manufacturers drew their workers from the millions of semiskilled immigrants who had arrived in that city in the first two decades of the twentieth century. These largely Italian and Jewish immigrants provided cheap labor in the city's "sweatshops," where they worked for incredibly long hours under remarkably cramped conditions for very little wages. Organized in 1900, the International Ladies Garment Workers Union set out to organize this enormous and disparate workforce. ("Ladies" in the union's name referred to the kind of garments made (that is, shirtwaists, dresses, underwear) and not to the gender of the workers—though a majority of garment workers were in fact women.) Two strikes, both in New York City, made the union: the first, in 1909, by twenty thousand shirtwaist workers, most of them female, and another in 1910, by fifty thousand cloak-makers, most of them male. As a result of these two successful strikes, by the start of World War I nearly four hundred thousand workers had joined the ILGWU, and working conditions had improved markedly.

In the 1920s, however, the ILGWU suffered from bitter political infighting and a disastrous 1926 cloak-makers strike that left the union with only forty thousand members and deeply in debt. Unlike most other unions and workers, however, the ILGWU managed to take advantage of the National Industrial Recovery Act and its promise of union recognition and collective bargaining for all workers. During a general strike in 1933, some two hundred thousand workers joined the ILGWU, making it one of the strongest and most progressive unions in the country. Because it organized across the garment industry, too, including both skilled and semiskilled workers, the ILGWU pioneered a form of industrial unionism, which predisposed it to play an influential role in the formation of the CIO in the second half of the 1930s.

From its beginnings, but especially in the 1930s, the ILGWU also devoted considerable resources to workers' education. Most famously, the union financed composer Harold Rome's *Pins and Needles,* an unexpectedly popular 1937 musical about exploited but defiant and romantic women garment workers performed by ILGWU union members themselves. The ILGWU also maintained several Unity Centers in and around New York City, including an enormous summer school complex for workers in upstate New York. These schools offered classes in everything from the English language to economics, art, literature, music, drama, philosophy, and history.

Perhaps not surprisingly, then, *Justice,* the newspaper of the ILGWU, also published a great deal of poetry and nurtured a number of regularly contributing garment poets. It published poems by the inscrutable but seemingly ubiquitous Mr. Modestus, just as it gave space to Arturo Giovannitti, the poet and legendary organizer of the 1912 IWW-led Lawrence, Massachusetts, textile strike. It also published many lesser-known or unknown poets, including the substantial work of Miriam Tane. Unlike other poets in this collection, Tane frequently used more self-consciously modern poetic techniques—open form, image, metaphor, symbol—to create complex, at times surrealistic poems about sweatshops, the city, consumerism, the ongoing and impending wars in Europe and Asia, and the redeeming possibilities of nature.

In a Garment Factory

Nahum Yood

In deafening clatter of motors
That turn the powerful wheel—
Low over machines bend the workers,
Like riders on horses of steel.

The horses are running and racing,
But not in the open God's space;
They swallow the long miles of cotton,
Of velvet, of silk, and of lace.

And crouched are the men in the saddles—
Imperious in the command . . .
And strained are the eyes and the muscles,
Yet quick and precise is the hand.

Thus day after day they are riding
And racing their horses of steel,
In deafening clatters of motors
That turn the powerful wheel.

From Justice, *April 1934.*

The Final Installment

Arturo Giovannitti

He lay in the blue-and-silver parlor of the royal suite of the great hotel
Full-stretched on the shivering rug, a thin ribbon of blood streaming out of
his left nostril,
His right hand half closed in a whimsical wink to the young sun,
His great thewed hands half open, giving back all his possessions—his
dream, his life and his revolver.

He had played his game manfully, observing all rules, and he had lost.
And now he lay there paying his last installment in full
To the pale little mob that had come to cash in on their hope and his moil.[1]
And the little mob that had been bought free from worry for a little while
With the tired eyes and the wilted souls of young girls he had conjured into
yellow coupons,
The little mob that worshipped the Great Forgiver and never had cast any
stones
Now waited for the scavenger of the Law to turn out the pockets of this last
peddler of salvation
Who had failed for ten million dollars to gain one farthing of peace.

They glowered at him with baneful eyes distorted by hate,
With a sullen fury against Death that had cheated them of revenge,
From a fuming hot clod of earth where once their heart sang psalms and
drinking ditties.
Yet, were he alive, or could he still be revived by the unspewed froth of their
mouths,
They would still cringe before him, still believe in the magic of his words,
Still pray that the alchemy of his brain transmute their inanity into gold
And their cowardice into valor and defiance.

The painted ladies, the lawyers, the doctors, the ministers, the God-fearing
savers of money (savers of courage, savers of love, savers of pity and all
hot lusts of life)

---

1. drudgery, hard work.

Jeered at him and cursed him, roiling the sweet summer air with impotent
    shouts made righteous by the drunken nods of the Law;
And one gnome shook his fist at him, and a braver one almost touched the
    bronze sandals of Glory by kicking the soles of his feet
(He swerved his leg on time from the lean jaw for fear of the lightning still
    unspent in his eyes and the thunder still echoing in his mouth)
And they babbled among themselves strange anathemas and infamies,
    invoking ancient powers of occult wrath and destruction, harrying
    Heaven and Hell with drooling incantations,
Ignobly defeated, guideless without this dead guide,
And a corpse became the emblem of their lives.

But facing this corpse, stolid as a sentry at attention,
A worker stood up with a pick on his arms
That glowed like a fiery saber.
He had failed a thousand times before, but was still girt for the fray
As he mourned in his self-slain neighbor
Perhaps a foe he no longer could slay,
And perhaps a lost comrade when the world turns his way
And every day sweated in labor
Will be a grand Labor Day.

From Justice, *September 1934. Both "The Final Installment" as well as "All-Fighter's Day"
(below) are by Arturo Giovannitti. Loosely affiliated with the International Workers of the
World, Giovannitti gained national fame from his role in the 1912 Lawrence, Massachusetts,
textile strike. During the course of that strike, a young woman was killed by the state militia.
Both Giovannitti and Joe Ettor, another IWW organizer, were arrested and charged with mur-
der, even though neither of them had been present when the shooting occurred. Ettor and Gio-
vannitti served a year in prison before a jury found them innocent. Once out of prison, Gio-
vannitti contributed poetry and essays to various left-wing journals such as* Masses, *the*
Liberator, New Masses, *and several Italian-language political journals. In the 1920s and
1930s, he helped establish an affiliate of the International Ladies Garment Workers Union,
Local 89—the Italian Dress Makers Union. Throughout the 1930s, he contributed poems to
the ILGWU newspaper,* Justice. *Like many of his poems, "The Final Installment" is a surreal,
at times allegorical poem whose meaning remains somewhat ambiguous. It may or may not
help to know that when he included it in his* Collected Poems, *Giovannitti titled the poem
"The Bankrupt's Suicide."*

Freedom

Martha Stevenson

No work for me in the shop today,
So out into the street I run,
Out from darkness into the sun,
Like a child at school released for a day,
Free as the winds that blow over the sea,
Gay as a peasant's dancing tune,
My whole being astir
With my unexpected liberty.
A day for myself to come and go
And do as I will; bask in sunlight,
Walk the wooded trails, think the thoughts
Welling up in me, be alive
As I can never be when chained
To my machine inside four ugly walls.

But I feel my pocket
And count the little money that is there,
And a fear grips me—
A fear that lingers and grows.
What of the morrow?
Will I be free again?
Oh call it not freedom
To be out upon the streets
Without bread.
And I hope and I pray for work
On the coming day. I pray, oh sin,
To be a slave once more.

And as I walk,
Foreboding gnaws at my heart,
Consuming my joy.
This shadow is over my head
Like a fog
When it holds down the dense black smoke
And darkens and chokes all that breathes,

It makes the sun to shine less brightly.
And soon I wonder—
Is this a holiday at all,
Or would I not rather be chained
To my machine.
And then my spirit rallies
To pour down a thousand curses
Upon the poverty that crushes
The joy I felt at being free,
That robbed me of my holiday
And cast a black storm cloud
Over the morning sunshine.

From Justice, *March 1, 1935. The poem was accompanied by the following note from the editor: "In the last issue of 'Justice' we described the type of life and experience that led Martha Stevenson from a New England farm into a New York dress shop and the working class movement. This is one of her poems. It probes sensitively the mixed feelings that come to the worker on an unexpected "day off." 'Justice' looks forward to printing more of her poems and those of other Union members who are sifting their experience and using them as themes.—Ed." Despite this welcome, Stevenson never published another poem in the newspaper.*

The I.L.G.W.U.

Max Press

Out of the twilight of the sweatshops,
Where the black machines drove death into the brain—
From the places of pain and toil and hunger,
We have won to a cleaner life again.

Our blood has run in the streets of the cities,
We have known the dungeon, the club and the fire,
In the days when we froze on the picket line
And faced the red-handed men of hire.

From the ruin and deaths of the "Triangle" fire,[1]
And the blood and sweat of Nineteen-Ten,[2]
We have built our union and closed our ranks—
And can hold up our heads like women and men.

Since the broken ranks of 'Twenty Six,
The road has been hard and the years have been long,
But we have stood our ground and kept the faith—
And we stand two hundred thousand strong.

We have broken the doors of the sweatshops,
And our locals reach from sea to sea,
And if our hearts are strong and our hands are clean
Ours is the ultimate victory.

We will win by the faith of the martyrs
Who stood the test when our numbers were few,
And we march with the sun upon banners
Of the I.L.G.W.U.

From Justice, *May 15, 1935.*

---

1. On March 25, 1911, a fire broke out on the top floors of the Triangle Shirt Waist Company, a sweatshop in Manhattan's Greenwich Village. By the time the fire was over, 146 of the 500 employees, mostly young women under the age of twenty, had died horrific deaths, either being trapped in the burning building or from jumping out of windows.
2. In July 1910, the ILGWU conducted one of its first strikes, involving some fifty thousand cloak-makers.

We talk of progress

Mr. Modestus

We talk of progress:
As though there were some goal—
Our path a measured route toward a terminal station.
A long view of history shows no constant climb or direction—
Rather appear the records of great cycles of continuous motion—
Involving smaller cycles of change and rise and fall.

This continent within 150 years has passed one cycle—
Pioneering began at Jamestown and Plymouth Rock—
Ending in Oklahoma, Oregon, and Texas.
Letters—that rode on ponies 200 years ago—
Have leaped to steam—the automobile—and the airplane—
Signals that spoke in smoke-waves—sparked on sun-beams—
Clicked through a wire—now register on universal waves of power.
Hand-power in a hoe—horse-power at a plow—
Steam-power on a rail-road—electric current on a wire—
But serve to introduce use to free-flying power—
Out toward the sun.

But in caverns of East India records dating back 300 millenniums—
Tell of flying navies in the air over Asia—
Of marvelous cities where now are sunken desert plains—
Of world-wide empires—whose seats of power are buried—
Deep under oceans whose depths we do not know as yet.
Mesopotamian plains are but cemeteries of civilizations gone.
Alexander stood at the peak—between Greece's rise and fall.
A Caesar marked the point in time where rising Rome began to sink.

In 476 A.D. the hordes overthrew Constantinople—
Between that day and 1492—when Columbus saw America first—
Stretched a thousand years of blackness—the Dark Ages.
Libraries were burned—and lost—
Nations were torn apart—stark war stalked across the lands of Europe—
Plague, pestilence and battle, ignorance, greed and lust—
Were the controlling powers of human destinies.

Then Spanish galleons brought argosies from Peru—
A Galileo saw the movements of constellations—
Gutenberg multiplied libraries with his type and press—
Philosophers followed commerce—opened minds of nations—
Secrets of alchemists became mechanics' tools—
Swift ships robbed oceans of their mysteries—
Long-buried forests then gave back in coal—
Concentrated power they gathered from the sun—
Pouring it in steam—by wheels and darting levers—
Through hammers, knives, saws, drills, bobbins and looms,
To lift a race through poverty, up from barbarism—

Into the half-light of an age of mechanisms—
Whither—?

Is it only a turning wheel?
Did October, 1929,[1] but mark the high point of a cycle?
Is it but just a Profit System—swinging on—
To mark another cycle?
Or can we here, like Pilgrim Fathers bold—
Mark out, and chart, and plan—another age to come?
Is it still morning in the Day of Steel?
Or has the noon passed—so that we face a setting sun?

From Justice, *August 1, 1935.*

1. October 24, 1929 (known as Black Thursday), the day the New York Stock Exchange crashed, an event considered to be one of the leading causes of the Great Depression.

It's a stick-up!

Mr. Modestus

It's a stick-up!
Haile Selassie,[1] you are about to be trimmed—
Chief of Police caught Benito in the act, and uncovered him—
Benito says: I've a dynamite plant under your City Hall—
Let me alone or I'll blow up the whole European works!
But before that I'll blast all your best war ships—
My desperate air-men will gladly die to clear the Mediterranean—
After that even Hitler's war gods don't know what will happen!

This international gun-man has the whole police-force buffaloed—
Japan got away with the same kind of thing in Manchuoko—[2]
That makes it "right" for Italy to practice on Abyssinia—[3]

1. Emperor of Ethiopia from 1930 to 1974. In 1935, Italy, under Benito Mussolini, invaded Ethiopia. In 1936, Selassie would be forced to flee to British protection.
2. In 1931, Japan invaded Manchuria and the following year renamed it Manchukuo (Modestus spells it "Manchuoko"), which then became a nominally independent state controlled by the Japanese.
3. Original name of Ethiopia.

Getting good training for whatever job is next in the dossier—
One good treaty broken deserves another!
England and France will do most of the real fighting, if any—
The little members of the League of Nations[4] will not—cannot—
So French Laval communicates his case of chronic jitters to John Bull
    Hoare—[5]
While Italian women fork over their wedding rings, for the gold.

Nobody wants any more world-war—
Except Mussolini, and Hitler, and Nippon—[6]
And perhaps—Stalin, when the time is ripe enough—
But, if Italy could be put out of the running, somehow—
Who would defend the Danube valley against Hitler's legions?
Could Russia even protect her Ukrainian grainfields from Germany?—
With Japan already thundering at her Mongolian borders?
Laval prefers to have Italy spending her armies in Abyssinia—
Rather than storming the southern Alps into France!

There have been other tests of Democracy in the world's history—
Some of them before the Dark Ages—
One was met when the Spanish Armada was smashed in England's
    Channel—[7]
Another was settled between Bunker Hill and Yorktown—[8]

Many said another victory came out of Flanders Fields—[9]
But while seeds of democracy were planted in the League of Nations—
Corps of dictatorship have sprouted also from Versailles—[10]

---

4. International organization formed at the conclusion of World War I to promote peace and security and avoid another world war. However, the League of Nations proved unable to stop or even slow the invasions, violence, and treaty violations in Europe in the 1930s and shortly thereafter collapsed.

5. "French Laval" refers to Pierre Laval, who was premier and foreign minister of France in 1935–36. "John Bull Hoare" refers to Sir Samuel Hoare, foreign secretary for Britain beginning in 1935. Together, they proposed a settlement to halt the Italian conquest of Ethiopia, widely seen as an appeasement of Mussolini.

6. Japan.

7. In 1588, English ships defeated the fleet sent by Spain, under Philip II, to invade the country and overthrow the Protestant Elizabeth I.

8. The opening and closing campaigns of the American Revolution.

9. Site of some of the deadliest battles of World War I; hundreds of thousands of soldiers died and were buried there.

10. Versailles, France, where the 1919 treaty that ended World War I and established the League of Nations was signed.

While Nippon's hands were loosed and strengthened during Europe's
    agony—
Today it seems that all the weapons of democracy have been impounded—
Intelligence, invention, communication, skill of hand and brain—
Are being chained and dragged at the chariot wheels of conquest.

The essence of power is: power controlled—
Co-operation of human minds and hands has been the source original—
The discipline and control of these have generated power of Nations—
But always these have disintegrated and fallen prey to lesser powers—
When the Dictator finished his period.

To gather, instruct, co-ordinate and integrate human power—
To operate mass production of intelligence—
To generate a mass control through self-control—
This is the pattern of democracy!
A Nation thus constructed would be impregnable—
Given required resources of land and minerals—
Lacking these factors of control, nations resort to dictatorships!
Nearest to all of filling this prescription—
The American people stand today facing the old enigma of the ages—
No mere dictatorship, or class, or group, or single mind—
Can meet this test we see approaching.

From Justice, *January 1, 1936.*

On Hearing a Negro Spiritual

Jessie Carter

Not from the servant sheltered in the house
Could come this freighted music, nor from them
Whose hands were taught to whip the master's horse
And lay the family silver on fine linen;
Not from the stolen shackled to the hulk
Of some swift slave ship, widowed from his tribe,
Seasick and bloody, too reduced to sulk

At death upon the waters or contrive
Music like this half pattern of a creed,
Half of a race in bondage alienated,
Who swapped their antelopes for milk white steed
Drawing a low-swung chariot, but mated
Words to the drum throb muffled to the ear
That hostile tribes might seek and never hear.

From Justice, January 15, 1936. The poem is almost certainly a reference to James Weldon Johnson's famous poem, "O Black and Unknown Bards."

All-Fighters Day

Arturo Giovannitti

I

Oh you, who stand grim and ready in the sudden eclipse of your day,
You with the rudderless heart, lovers and rovers of storms,
Whose torch is the lightning, whose goal is the lair of spent hurricanes,
Lend ear to us, listen and answer, for ours alone is this day and we teem
    with all the tomorrows.
We know you will not be disturbed if broken and fierce and obscure and
    without peace is our message.
For your lips also are hardened with sneers and battle calls,
And your blood that has not been infected with the sacred vaccine of the
    lamb
Shall foam now like a strong must in the raised goblets of spring,
To warm the old heart of the earth and redden the cheeks of the gods.

II

My friend, I and my comrades, Men and She-Men, have elected you
To the magnificent feast of this last baptism of War,
And today you will be initiated in this mad brotherhood of ours
If you but ask to come in by striking your sword on the door.
Whatever the host you are serving, whatever the name of your cause,

If nobler your flag seems to you when nearer you see the red death
Of those whom the rabble calls fools, and men and history call heroes,
Then you are even as we, and surely one day we shall meet
And clasp our gauntleted hands on the main highway of life.

III

May you then, with or without us, know all the furies and struggles
Of the spirit that never weakens, of the flesh that never wearies,
And all the plans and the woes and the blows and the wounds of the world;
And hunger and thirst and cold that make the body twin to the earth.
May you see on the lips of your bride the same anguished smile that first
        chained our destiny to that of our warrior women,
And the cowardly fear of your shadow on the brow of your best trusted
        friend,
And the tears of your mother, the mightiest army to rout,
And the blank stare of your children, the thickest wall to break through;
And your own loneliness of him who leads and can never turn back,
Nor stop, nor ask anyone for the road to the summit,
The only place where is rest.
Let the long hours of waiting come to you, and the endless aeons of desire;
And let yourself know hope when hope is less easy than despair,
And despair when its bludgeons strike harder than the hammers of faith,
And may you also, brave Friend (cruel or craven is he who denies this)
In those collected hours when return to you the silent messengers of your
        heart that have tarried behind your lusts and the dust of your feet,
May you also know the tears that are neither sorrow nor weeping,
Nor regret nor remorse, nor any backwash of the past,
But the pillaged trophies of your soul that has surrendered nothing in the
        red sunset of defeat,
Nor has gained aught in the chilly dawn of conquest
Save a sharp stone to sit on and a view of the battle-scarred field!

IV

Strange friend, whoever you are, gregarious or solitary,
Preserver of antique lores or wrecker of ancient wrongs,
Or asserter of earth-born rights, or confessor of new-found truths,
If you receive this message and return it even as it came,

You shall not have the peace of the peaceful nor the happiness of the
    happy,
But you shall have Force and with Force you shall be nearer to Wisdom,
And you shall find your true comrade, your guide and your servant—
    Yourself,
And feel no longer alone.

V

And lo! You shall eat black bread and bitter olives with the ancient hunger
    of the athletes,
And you shall drink the rain of the storms and the water of the cataracts
    with the magnificent thirst of the Titans;
And you shall sleep on the bare earth, watched by the fires of volcanoes, the
    ample sleep of the Cyclops;
And in your sleep you shall walk with the gods, and in your waking hours
    you shall discourse with the sages and converse with the heroes;
And you shall have whole and unsullied the body and the soul of your
    woman, forever beyond the fear of death or new desire;
And your children shall grow around you nimble and swift and hard like
    the colts and the wolflings,
And you shall be unafraid of the heights and of the deeps, like the eagle and
    the shark, being of uneatable flesh.
Aye, and men shall lay traps and nets for you and you will not live long nor
    placidly,
Even unto the end which comes alike to a sun and to a worm.
And what imports the most, my friend,
you will not die in bed amidst flickering tapers and odors of sanctity, and
    cries and wailings and benedictions.

But your spirit, ravished in the arms of the tempest, shall be extolled in the
    triumphal paean of the wind, above the ramparts of time, unto the
    glory of the unbeholdable light!

From Justice, *May 1, 1936.*

What Do You Build?

Syde Waller

In what cloud of vague thought
Can you call yourselves free?
Ye serf,—their pockets fraught
With fruit,—of Slavery!
O,—is this,—that kind of freedom
Lincoln taught?

I hear a hammer thump!
What do you build,—Worker?
What tyrannical pomp
Shall reside,—what shirker
Shall taste its warmth,—while ye
to your dungeons limp!

What talent do they bring?
O, how do they do good,—
That from your veins they wring,—
Like leeches,—drink your blood?
'Twas Shelley said this,—and great-
er, didst never sing![1]

Ye needle warming clothes,—
Can't wear,—it's on their shelf!
Ye plant,—the flower grows.
Yet after led,—they steal the odor
from the rose!

From Justice, *February 15, 1937.*

---

1. From Percy Bysshe Shelley's "To the Men of England": "Wherefore feed and clothe and save, / From the cradle to the grave, / Those ungrateful drones who would / Drain your sweat—nay, drink your blood?" Beyond this direct allusion, Waller reworks Shelley's more famous poem.

Labor Stage

Hilda W. Smith

Out of the shops where your machines are whirring,
Out of your bitter, undefeated youth,
From years of basting, stitching, tucking, shirring,
Speak, garment workers, dramatize the truth![1]

Speak for those others, those whose voices mumble;
Too tired to hope, too dauntless to despair;
As amateurs in half-learned parts they stumble,
Rehearse these others. Make them, too, aware.

Let daily bread be salted with your laughter;—
Reality made pungent with a jest;—
Let music, in fresh rhythm, follow after;
The sober facts sung gaily with a zest.

The doors stand wide. The audience is seated.
Stretch your dramatic fiber, pricked with pins.
Let labor speak its lines; truth undeleted.
Ring up the curtains! Now the play begins!

From Justice, *May 1, 1938. Hilda W. Smith (1888–1972) was a graduate of Bryn Mawr College and later a dean at that same institution. In 1921, she was named director of the Bryn Mawr Summer School for Women Workers, an early and influential effort in the field of workers' education. In 1933, she was appointed a specialist in workers' education under the Federal Emergency Relief Administration and founded numerous centers for the training of unemployed workers and teachers.*

---

1. In 1934, the ILGWU acquired the Princess Theatre, a small Broadway theater on West Thirty-ninth Street. Renamed the Labor Stage in 1937, the ILGWU produced Harold Rome's labor musical *Pins and Needles* there in the same year. With a cast comprised entirely of ILGWU members, the musical quickly developed into a national phenomenon, running for 1,108 performances, at the time the longest-running Broadway show ever.

To Whom It May Concern . . .

Max Press

You read your paper, muse awhile, doze, and forget
The fields of Death have many, many acres yet;
That Earth turns on an axis oiled by blood and sweat.

The good years are brief and the pits of doom are deep;
Inward the waves of horror, hate, and ruin creep—
How can I rouse you from the tragedy of sleep?

Does not the nightmare come: of trenches in the rain,
The mute faces of boys bewildered in their pain,
And the terrible, staring, blind eyes of the slain?

Earth waits beneath the menace of a ghastly sky;
Wide, wide her fields of death and desperation lie—
If you awake we live, and if you sleep we die.

From Justice, *May 1, 1938.*

Spring

Miriam Tane

Spring, anciently new, eternally green
comes to the city, like peace after war.

And as the moist greenness of Spring
warms and stirs the spent bodies
of those whose hands urge endless streams of
stitches from clattering machines,
they strain against the iron seams of the
factory, joining the fabric of their lives
to their machines with threads of steel.

For them
there is no spring—
no spring
for them.

For them
clusters of cherries, flowers and apple trees
in crimson, yellow, purple, blue and green
blossom on the shabby smocks of pale women.

For them
the joyous smells of Spring,
of yesterday's and tomorrow's springs,
are heavy, airless shop smells.

For them
the glistening rings of dew on petal ears
are beads of sweat oozing down
their cheeks and necks and arms,
falling on the gaudy colored prints.

For them
the glint of the morning and the setting-sun
is the electric bulb, hot and angry,
fretting the eyes and dripping lead on the lids.

For them
the throats of birds are silent
and only the frenzied snap of electric power
storms through the machines.

But just as Spring rises throbbing with new life
from the wastes of old winter,
So life's winter shall sink into the earth—
and life's Spring rise throbbing with new life.

And Spring anciently new, eternally green
shall come to the factory,
like peace after war.

From Justice, *April 1, 1939. Miriam Tane (1916–2007) was born on June 7, 1916, in New York City. Her parents, Samuel and Shifra Tane, left the town of Tarnapol, in present-day Poland, and settled in Manhattan, where her father worked as a garment presser in the city's sweatshops and her mother raised a family of eight children. Tane graduated from James Monroe High School in New York City and briefly attended Hunter College, which she left at the age of twenty to enter the labor movement. In 1936, she joined Local 22 of the International Ladies Garment Workers Union, the home for the militant, multiethnic, multiracial, and largely female workers who stitched dresses in and around Manhattan. Tane became active in Local 22's Education Department and eventually took jobs in garment factories in New York and across the industrial Northeast, surreptitiously helping workers to organize locals of their own. In 1946, Tane left the labor movement and married Mitchell Siporin, a WPA artist who painted several post office murals and would later go on to direct the fine arts program at Brandeis University.*

Factory Windows

Miriam Tane

Towering
are the stout-sided, fat-bellied factories
like tawny-tinged, earthenware jugs, stained
with soot, and tightly juxtaposed
along streets of slow-pacing
crowds, sluggish as serpents
in the sun.

Recurring
batches of men and women are thrust
into their bulging necks and disgorged

only when their sweat has irrigated a
soil of vibrating steel
to bring forth
harvests which they
never reap!

And over
the grimy, factory-roofs' face, pockmarked
with pebble stones, the sky is blue,
minty salve!

The sky, as
fresh as water from an earthborn
spring
flecked with color of ripe apricot as if a
vein had burst in the swollen sun,
belongs to the others, to those who
own the factory windows, from which
these, humped over their machines, with
shoulders round almost as their twirling
Spools of thread, sighing furtively,
glimpse the sky

And envy
the brown, soft, supple smoke forever
trailing out of the factory into the
clouds, like crumpled parachutes, lost in
endless space, and air, and light, and never
coming back!

When the will
of each shall coalesce as one, grow hard
as rock with which to shatter the pane,
then, the time for envy will have passed,
for not only the window, but the sky stretching
beyond all shall belong to all, and with its ripping
thunder and teeming rain sweep the world clean for a clear,
windless dawn!

From Justice, _May 15, 1939._

Stitching Machine

Miriam Tane

Backbone hooked to sweat-browned chairs
inseparable as wounds to flesh and tears,
imprisoned like cloth between hands and shears
leashed to blind machines (like human hounds),—
spluttering
Esperanto of electric sounds.

Held tightly, as needle points of steel,
impelled
propelled by the constant whirling wheel
grips loose edges in unbreaking seams,—
seaming as if in unwaking dreams.

To the living, riveted to compliance
like Earth to
space, to those who know no need of defiance,—
What is Time?—to the seamstresses
and seamsters
of the world's sundry trousers and dresses?

A stitching machine,—almost like
to themselves
grinding out pieces of time, like
stitches—driven by the mind's slow power,—
with winding thread,—second, minute, hour . . .

And new garments by new living are spun
for stitching for the living's never done!

From Justice, *July 1, 1939.*

Dignity

Miriam Tane

Soft, folded body
forms an acute
angle to sewing machine,
and from tensioned limbs
leap movements minutely
calculated, hoarded from
defeating time.

And as the void of listless
day widens into release
of night, the inert become
catapulting crowds seeking
the swift-running course
to the boroughs. Tide of
the going and the coming
is harnessed to the subway.
The days are similar as
one grain of salt to
another, and tomorrow is
formless to them who hate
what they are, yet have no
breath to sigh for what
they are not.

Lymph of lassitude
seeps into the body's
marrow, like rainwater
sogging into the under-
brown of crusty earth.
The songs men sing
remain somewhere in
vacuous objectivity.

But he who takes their stitches
to market
for gold with which to buy
sun, space, and air,
muses
In sun-yellow sands:
"Ah, yes, grateful they should
be to me,
I gave them dignity!"

From Justice, *August 15, 1939.*

Evacuations

Miriam Tane

I must evacuate my mind
of the sand-bagged city
waiting with arched back
for the bomb boom,
in black.

I must mute the magpie city
screaming bullet headlines
on wires strung through clouds
down open mouths
of crowds.

I must gouge out the neon eye
of the city from the
mind's marquee, for
in the city there
is war—in the city where
peace is a bread crumb on
the viscous ancient waters.

I must stop my ears with country
side, graft it to my ear
like soft woman breast
to muffle all
the rest.

I must find music intimate as
a hand, and know again the
moist manner of rain,
birdfeet on the
terrain.

I must sit in shadowed space, wear-
-ing soft mittens of non-
remembrance, cool as glass
through which, non-heating,
suns pass—in the country where
the color of silence is green,
and not the color of death!

From Justice, *October 1, 1939.*

Headline Fugitive

Miriam Tane

For two or three legal, American pennies you can buy from your local
    newsstand, fresh, newsprint smelling death by
    bombing
    blasting
    submarining
    airraiding!
Livid, living, burning news flesh!

Newspaper bowing before disaster like an important guest.
Disaster relayed by gram, graph,
    and photo,
    splaying into the eyes and the
    face of the you who has

two or three, legal American pen-
nies to spend
> on the news
> of the day
> in the world
> of today!

And for the same copper sum,
> to relieve the tireless tattoo
> of the newsticker on the brain,
> you can turn away from
> front page frenzy by
> turn-turning the pages to where
Alice Bluegroan takes the loveless
> to her columnar bosom, and neatly
> mends all broken hearts
> with the adhesive of advice;

And where America's one and only
> largest department store makes a
> bombshell announcement
> of the
> biggest
> sale in the
history of
> Clothes pins!

From Justice, *January 15, 1940.*

Day in Technicolor

Miriam Tane

After the six-day, week-by-week, endurance test, race, fight to the finish for
    a bread-and-butter prize;
After the sixth day of bringing home the bacon, of end-meeting-end. Of
    living in the space of a budget of answering all the asking who asked to
    be paid;

After the beating of the other little guy at his own little game, and the
    pulling of the fast one, and the dog eating dog,
And the knowing of the ropes, and the tricks, and ins and outs, and the
    knowing of the people who know the people with the connections.
After the selling of all the saleable articles, except static, rainwater, thunder
    and torn paperbags,
Anything that can be wrapped, shipped, or COD'd or returned for a larger
    size, or envied or borrowed from the neighbors;
Anything that can make the register ring like wedding bells;
After six days, that start if you keep waking to aliveness every morning, at
    seven, eight, or nine; end at five, six, seven, time and a half for
        overtime, (maybe)
Comes Sunday, Technicolor day of the week; day of rest, relaxation on
    which the nation reads the comics, want ads, situations wanted,
        business opportunities which knock but once;
Gets indigestion from overeating;
And a nation-wide hookup of Charlie
McCarthy[1] to quiet their coffee
Nerves.

From Justice, *March 1, 1940. In the 1930s, the Technicolor Corporation developed and patented a process for making color movies. By sensitizing strips of black and white film to a certain color, infusing the film with that color, and then running the strips synchronously, Technicolor could produce an integrated, high-quality color image.*

---

1. The name of the puppet Edgar Bergen used in his popular radio ventriloquist act.

Night Fog

Miriam Tane

Out from the movies where
    a boy-meets-girl and a
gangster-meets-trouble, double
    feature bill, trebled by screeno,[1]
is a go-to-sleep song for a
    Nineteen Forty brain:

---

1. A variant of bingo played in motion picture theaters.

Out from the meeting halls
    where amendments and
amendments to the amendments
    are moved and seconded
in and out of order, and throats
    are hoarse with
smoke and dare-and-do slogans:

Out from the lecture halls where
    I-told-you-so gentlemen diagnose
the future of disaster, and draw
    black little crosses for
Europe on a map, dead as your
    last night's radio program:

And out into the night-streets
find the fog waiting,
soft and smooth
as smoke-brown hair,
except where the lamplights show,
like old, ivory-yellow teeth!

Find the fog walking
before and behind, sitting
on doorsteps and telegraph wires,
slowing the quick,
come-and-get-it wink of neon
signs in the dissolving sky,
and kissing the smiling faces
of the pretty girls on billboards.

And ask perhaps of the night
What is it about a haunting
dreamdrift of a fog
that makes you so mixed-up happy?

From Justice, *April 18, 1940.*

Blue-Eyed Pigeon

Miriam Tane

. . . Hands mechanical
over seams, over threads,
over buttons,
thimbles of pain
in our fingertips,
pincushions of pain
at our backs,

and the mind
sometimes unreels
automatic
like a fish line into the sea,
as a camera by an in-the-
gloaming ghost making
mad, like-in-a-dream pictures . . .

. . . a madman sitting
with his legs crossed
around his neck
sucking on a rind of
lemon, and smelling
a white, green-stemmed rose

. . . or a blue-eyed pigeon
wearing a gay, Spring hat,
smoking a Camel with a
jade-green holder . . .
it happens to me
I know . . .
especially now when
Spring leaps in
through the windows.

From Justice, *May 15, 1940.*

Parent Prayer

Miriam Tane

Be frightened that your son
is five-ten tall
and his feet aren't flat,
his chest expansion four;
that he has thirty-two teeth
and a good appetite,

has two strong arms,
and two swift legs; has eyes
that can talk tender to a girl
and see a blind bullet to its
flesh; has ears that can hear
"I love you" in a voice and the
murderous hate in a bomb; has
nostrils for the scent of
tapering tulip beds, machine
gunpowder and poison vomit gas.

Pray for the gift to your son
of a physical handicap to keep
him from killing and killed;
pray for a glandular deficiency,
blurred double vision, or a
pair of fallen arches; a low
blood count, high blood pressure,
or a limb insufficiency like a
finger, or a toe, or an ear.

Listen for a murmur in his heart;
a ringing in his ears;
a hacking cough at midnight;
a wheeze in his breathing;
or a cry of delirium.

Sing when you call the doctor and
dance to the music of his diagnoses!

From Justice, *June 15, 1940.*

Morning

Miriam Tane

Morning is a casual spade
uprooting my body pinioned
in the webbed warmth of night,
returning, returning intent
like a skilled shiny insect
foraging the rosebud's heart.

Idly sometimes I wonder.how it
would look suddenly in the newspapers,
were I to snatch morning
from the sleeping city's step,
wrench it from its socket,
turning morning off
like a faucet dripping
in a silent empty house . . .
and banish the clock unloading
the inert clattering hour.

From Justice, *August 1, 1940.*

Cafeteria

Miriam Tane

Bright solarium in glass wrapped
crowning night's ulcerated base,—
we seek community in cafeterias . . .
we step by accident on a
stage drenched in footlights.

People seem in costume here,
carrying their trays happily.

The ladies this year trim
their coats with tigerskins;
they wear their lips like bright
insects on the knuckled mouth,
the men are distant relatives
present on the arm like umbrellas.

The women with the nation's colors
on her patriotic bosom
suspends the ecstasy of a bite
into her hamburger to exclaim:
"—I'd simply die if Hitler
bombed our five and tens.—"

We sit for our portraits
in the mirrored mirrors answering
us with—"Not responsible
for personal property."

Finally, we lock the branches
of our loneliness like arms
and together we test our strength
against the revolving door.

From Justice, *January 1, 1941.*

International Sailors Union
(National Maritime Union of America)

In December 1935, leaders of the AFL-affiliated International Seamen's Union signed a contract with the New York–based American Steamship Company that continued the vast discrepancies in working conditions and wages between East Coast and West Coast seamen. As a result, rank-and-file East Coast seamen revolted, calling a series of strikes in the New York harbor opposed by both shipowners and the ISU. At an enormous rally in New York in 1937, the sailors split with the union and founded the CIO-affiliated National Maritime Union of America, which rapidly went on to organize almost all the East Coast–based shipping lines and sailors. While still part of the ISU, rank-and-file sailors started their own newspaper, the *Pilot*, which from the start printed poetry in almost every issue, much of it the work of the pseudonymous Forty Fathoms.

Eight Bells
Left Rudder

We've manned your death doomed rotten hulks
That you might profit gain,
And sailed from home not knowing if
We would return again;
Above a million watery graves
The angry billows roll
If sacrifice is freedom's price
We sure have paid the toll.

You've sent us o'er uncharted seas
To peddle pelf in marts,
In plague . . . infested lands and climes
And fever stricken parts,
We've faced the perils of the deep
For you each day and more.
And led the life a sailor must
While you stayed safe ashore.

But what has been your gratitude?
To us that served you well,
Each of your death doomed rotten hulks
Is still a floating hell.
From the press and from the pulpit
Your propaganda spreads.
To mislead and fool the public that
Our strike was called by "reds."

With Truth and Science on our side
And with the aid of Time,
There'll come a day when you must pay
For all your tyrant crime.
From San Francisco's Golden Gate
To Ambrose Channel Light[1]
With Federated Unity
We'll demonstrate our might.

From I.S.U. Pilot, *April 24, 1936. "Eight Bells" is midnight.*

---

1. Instead of a lighthouse, the southern entrance (Ambrose Channel) to the New York Harbor used a lightship, the Ambrose Channel Light.

For Seven Years I've Roamed the Seas

J. Freeman

For seven years I've roamed the seas
I've swabbed the deck upon my knees;
I've greased the stays, I've passed the coal,
And sweated in my glory hole.[1]

> *(And though I did my duty well,*
> *Many a skipper gave me hell;*
> *Many a mate has kicked my can—*
> *The privilege of a gentleman.)*

I've oiled the winches, steered the course,
The food I ate would kill a horse;
And when the month was done, they gave
Me fifty bucks for being slave.

> *(The gents who own the ships and me,*
> *They clip their coupons steadily;*
> *They scrub no deck, they haul no line,*
> *And yet their income's more than mine.)*

On the ship's bow I took my stand,
For weeks and weeks I saw no land;
And sick of man, and sick of beef,
My bones were crazy for relief.

> *(Owners of ships with stocks and bonds,*
> *They have their dark girls and their blondes;*
> *They can't think, when they drink their scotch,*
> *Like sailors think upon the watch.)*

Rolling from port to port I see
Other workers, slaves like me;
And as the years they roll along,
It seems to me there's something wrong.

---

1. Any small enclosed space in which unwanted items are stowed when clearing up decks.

(O gentlemen with tall silk hats,
And diamond rings and pearl-gray spats,
You won't be bosses very long,
When workers see there's something wrong.)

From I.S.U. Pilot, *June 25, 1937.*

Shipowners' "Days" . . .

Forty Fathoms

The wooden ships
And iron men
Will those days
Ever come back again?
The days of toil for little pay
When sailors had no word to say
The days when men who sailed the sea
Took no heed of their misery
Those were the days.

The wooden ships
And iron men
Who questioned not
May heaven send
Men's minds were then on wind and sail
On storm and calm or winter hail
On canvas drawing up aloft
Our profits rose with pickings soft
Those were the days.

Those were the days
Of sailor men
Whose only thought
Was Sea again
The long wild passage of the Horn

That made them wish they ne'er were born
The days of hardtack and salt horse
The maggots, weevils, shout and curse
Those were the days.

The good old days
Of docile men
Whose cans mates kicked
In shape again
Who bent their backs o'er icy yards
Whose deeds are sung by crackpot bards
Who fought with death for little pay
Earned all our gold, had not to say
THOSE WERE THE DAYS.

From I.S.U. Pilot, August 13, 1937. It may not shed much light on why the poet chose his pseudonym, but in nautical terminology, a fathom is a unit of six feet; "forty fathoms"—that is, 240 feet—often marks the line between shore and sea. Many ships towed a kind of anchor, forty fathoms long, called a kite, *which, upon striking bottom, rose to the surface to indicate the approach of shore.*

To the Seamen of the International Brigade

(And to HARRY HINES, former editor of the PILOT, killed in action at Brunete,[1] one year ago.)

Willie Sue Blagden

You who will not now
Take ship again for any other shore
Have laid the contradiction bare.
Your battle was for peace who died at war
Courageous and aware.
Adequate memorial will come.

---

1. On July 6, 1937, the Spanish Republican Army, including the International Brigades, launched a major offensive against the town of Brunete, just west of Madrid, which the Fascists used as a base for their siege of Madrid. The Republican soldiers made early progress, but eventually suffered heavy losses, some twenty-five thousand men.

When victory is won;
After the sky in Spain is clear
Of fascist bomb
And children may look upward without fear.²

Sleep well forever, comrades,
Quietly restore
The chemistry you'll use no more.

And you who will return,
Walk proudly in the sun!
Hold high your head!
Strong as our class is strong,
Steeled by the strength of our dead.

From I.S.U. Pilot, *July 29, 1938. On the Spanish Civil War, see note to "Madrid" in the Industrial Workers of the World section. In September 1936 the Soviet Comintern began organizing the International Brigades, some fifty-nine thousand volunteers from across Europe and North America who traveled to Spain to defend the Republic. The three thousand American volunteers— mostly workers, students, and teachers, nearly all Communists—formed the American Lincoln Battalion. Over the course of the war, over one-third of the American volunteers would die.*

---

2. At the beginning of the war, Hitler sent General Franco German aircraft fighters, together called the Condor Legion. The Condor Legion participated in all the major battles of the war, but also engaged in "carpet bombing" Republican cities, most famously the town of Guernica, which caused international outrage and inspired Pablo Picasso's painting of the same name. Inevitably, many children died during these bombing raids, and, in the hopes of shocking foreign governments into action, the Republicans published photographs of the dead children.

My Picket Card

Anonymous

A card I prize as souvenir
Enshrined in folder frame,
Gives number of my Union-book,
Department, and full name.
It shows exact amount of days
That I was on the "Line"—
And there is nought I value more
Than that old card of mine.

O be it far from me to boast—
And yet, I'm jolly proud—
Of that old card that tells the world
I mingled with that crowd,
Who did respond to Neptune's call
And gave of their support,
Aiding—in some little way
To hold the Union fort.

And as I gaze upon that card
Enclosed within its shrine,
We trudge through slush and mud
As picket-men with "sign."
And comes to mind the wintry nights,
And dreary afternoons,
The battles that were fought and won
With stooges, yeggs, and goons.

We dine again on "twatered soup"[1]
And three-day's old stale bread,
I see the strike-fires that we kept
By dock, and pier, and shed.
I hear the songs that then were sung,
The yarns we loved to tell,
And ring of youthful laughter as
The winter's snowflakes fell.

Again we give "off-duty time"
To picket line en masse,
Forgetting sect, and faith, and creed,
With only thought for "Class,"
And wonder to myself how come
There was no wrangling then?
Nor petty feuds and clashing cliques
Nor slander tongue, nor pen.

---

1. Could refer to "watered soup," that is, "watered-down soup."

And then, somehow, that sacred card
More somber thought revives,
As comes to me the memory
Of men who gave their lives,
And as I placed that souvenir
Back in its folder frame
I feel a gladness in my heart
That I had played the game.

From The I.S.U. Pilot, *January 20, 1939.*

Dreams 1914–1918

Forty Fathoms

Was it a dream!
The great, squat ugly ships
With turrets bristling
And roar from iron lips;
Destruction, Death
A-scurrying o'er the world
Hastening to a rendezvous
Where mankind's hopes are hurled!

The moon hangs over the sea tonight
Its full beams fill the sky
With mellow light—with mellow light
Too bad that I must die.

Was it a dream!
Those troopships striped and weird,
The camouflage which did not serve
To hide our human fears.
There's little room upon the deck,
And less in rat-filled trench;
Humans delivered to death's door
To die midst roar and stench.

Oh blossom time may come and go,
The summer is at hand
With smell of bay and clover.
There's none in No-Man's Land.[1]

Was it a dream!
The broken, shattered men
Their youth behind them
Who came back again;
Great Christ! the wrongs we suffered,
And the Woe!
What had we done
That men should suffer so.

The silver birches tremble with life
The Lake is a silver gleam
A startled doe leaps up in fright
In dugout mud I dream.

Was it a dream!
The bloodstained, tattered rags,
The broken skeletons,
And the limbs that drag
A metal Cross
To mock Eternal Woe
Pinned on my breast by fat, white hands
That Hell did never know.

It is no dream!
The ones for whom we die
Raise golden mansions
To the silent sky.
God damn their souls
Who thrive on flesh and blood
Though millions workers perish
Dying in the mud.

From I.S.U. Pilot, *December 15, 1939.*

---

1. The unoccupied land separating opposing armies.

Blind Justice
Forty Fathoms

Justice—should be merciful.
Justice—should be kind.
But how explain the bandage . . .
Is it that Justice is blind?[1]

The dead who fell on Spanish fields,
Who died for Liberty's glow
Can speak of unfeeling Justice—
They died and they should know.[2]

The millions dead of China
Murdered by steel we made,[3]
They see the mask that Justice wears
And now speak unafraid:

Aye! Justice wears a bandage
And profits tip her scales.
What's honor, justice, human lives!
Her slogan's "Lives for Sale."

From I.S.U. Pilot, *October 25, 1940.*

---

1. The poem draws on ancient (and contemporary) depictions of the figure of Justice that show her appearing with scales and a blindfold, supposedly to indicate impartiality.
2. On the Spanish Civil War, see note to "Madrid" in the Industrial Workers of the World section.
3. On the Japanese invasion of China, see note to "you work tomorrow" in the United Auto Workers section. Despite the atrocities Japan committed against China in the 1930s, the United States continued to sell it iron and steel, much of which, of course, made possible its attacks against China.

The Negro Seaman Speaks
Forty Fathoms

I AM A NEGRO!
White Brothers.
Listen to the Song of my Race!
From the burning land of Africa
We come—

History has known us
Through the dim ages of Time.
Before the written word—hieroglyphics
We erected pyramids!
Science was OURS!
From the African kraals[1]
Came councils, governments—
We were old, old,
And wise in wisdom
Before the white men came.

Babylon, Egypt, Carthage, the Moors,
Were a later day to us—
We gave you astronomy, agriculture,
Religion, irrigation—
We taught the World new methods
Created Life for All.
We gave you iron,
And in the hands of barbarians
This gave us death,
Wars, slavery, pillage, slaughter—
Sold in bondage.

And Now—
We slave with you, white brothers,
Side by side.
We built the South's plantations

---

1. Village.

Under the lash of Masters;
Men died—
White and Black alike
For Freedom—Liberty—
Buried in the self same graves
At Gettysburg.

Listen to our cry—white brothers—
For you are Brothers
Welded by labor's pangs.
We are a part of you—indivisible—
With common aims and hopes—
And common future.
We cannot live alone.
We need YOUR AID—YOU, OURS—
For WE ARE BROTHERS.

From I.S.U. Pilot, *November 6, 1940. Unlike many unions affiliated with the American Federation of Labor, unions affiliated with the CIO—especially left-leaning ones like the International Sailors Union and the United Auto Workers—made special efforts to appeal to black workers and to recruit African Americans as both members and officers (though the subject of unions and race remains much debated among historians of trade unionism in the 1930s). As in "The Negro Seaman Speaks," unions' appeal to African Americans often attempted to transcend racial differences by focusing on the mutual exploitation of workers, black and white alike.*

The Slogan

Forty Fathoms

I

The World cannot live
Half-slave and half-free!
Our warmongers shout
On land and on sea;
A golden slogan
For nefarious scheme
Betraying us as pawns
In imperialist dream.

II

You twist its true meaning
Of this slogan so old
To hurl us into holocaust
For the Masters of Gold!
In a cause of slave empires
Now at each other's throat,
Who on slavery exist
And on misery gloat.

III

Our fight against slavery,
True Labor replies,
Is HERE in AMERICA
And to hell with your lies—
Look on the slums
That lie at your hand!
Gaze on stark misery
Throughout our fair land!
Look on slave barriers;
The blacks and poor white
Barred from the ballot
Their electoral right!

IV

One third of a the Nation
Ill-housed, clad, and fed—[1]
Substandard conditions
For our vast living dead!
When you rave about slavery
To be smashed o'er sea
FIRST DO IT AT HOME
And with this WE AGREE.

---

1. From Franklin Delano Roosevelt's Second Inaugural Address in January 1937: "I see one-third of a nation ill-housed, ill-clad, ill-nourished."

And when WE HAVE WON
TRUE FREEDOM RIGHT HERE
Then, we'll think of slave empires
Who real Liberty fear.

V

And THIS is OUR answer
To your cravings for loot—
REAL FREEDOM must be Ours
ERE THIS SLOGAN BEARS FRUIT.

From I.S.U. Pilot, *1941.*

United Auto Workers

Automobiles emerged as one of the major industries in the United States in the second decade of the twentieth century, and from the start autoworkers made sporadic attempts to organize unions. Nearly all of those attempts—including a concerted effort in 1934—failed, having suffered from the AFL's insistence on separating skilled autoworkers like machinists and tool-and-die workers from the majority of unskilled, rank-and-file assembly line workers. To be sure, these attempts also failed because the big three automakers—Ford, GM, and Chrysler—worked harder and devoted more resources than perhaps any other companies in the world to keeping an "open shop" and preventing workers from forming unions.

In July 1936, though, the United Auto Workers of America left the craft-oriented AFL for the recently launched Congress of Industrial Organizations, which had pledged to organize all workers in an industry regardless of craft or skill or competing union jurisdictions. That move would prove the making of both the CIO and the UAW. By the start of 1937, the CIO and UAW would both score their first and most important victories when autoworkers in Flint, Michigan, occupied their General Motors factories and, after a dramatic, at times heroic sit-down strike that lasted well over a month, finally won union recognition. The UAW would soon reach a similar agreement with Chrysler, but, as much of the poetry demonstrates, the union encountered significantly more resistance from Henry Ford. Still, the outcome of the Flint sit-down strike, involving the capitulation of one of the largest and most anti-union employers in the country, inspired workers everywhere, many of whom would eventually follow the autoworkers' lead by sitting down on their jobs and demanding union recognition.

Between 1937 and 1941, workers at Flint, Dearborn (home of Henry Ford's enormous River Rouge complex), and many of the other major production centers across the country contributed hundreds of poems to their lively newspaper, the *United Auto Worker*. Those poems often took their inspiration from the grievances autoworkers suffered on the job. First, and perhaps primary among their shop floor grievances, workers resented the "speed-up," their term for the punishing rate of work made possible by the shift to assembly line production and principles of scientific management. In the poems that follow, the pseudonymous Poll's "pressure" reflects the crippling intensity of work in an auto factory, as do Ralph H. Marlatt's "Have you ever worked on a line puttin' out five thousand bodies a day?" and Tobie's "Fordism."

Second, as reflected in Poll's free-verse poem "you work tomorrow," workers railed against and feared the frequent and prolonged layoffs—necessitated by annual car model changes—that reduced their yearly wages and left them idle for months at a time. Without a system of seniority, foremen decided who would work and who would not, a system that led (or so workers believed, with some cause) to foremen abusing their power by playing favorites, rewarding toadies, and punishing "troublemakers"—that is, anyone who complained or supported the union.

Finally, workers objected to what we might call, for lack of a better term, the "fascism" that characterized working and living conditions in the automobile industry. General Motors, for example, employed hundreds of professional and amateur labor spies, who together infiltrated unions and eavesdropped on shop floor conversations, "ratting" on workers sympathetic to the union and leading other, potentially sympathetic workers to hide their interest for fear of losing their jobs. (Murray Roth's "A Stoolie's Lament" offers a satiric portrait of how this practice changed with the advent of the UAW.) For his part, instead of spies, Henry Ford relied on Harry Bennett and his sinister "Service Department" to keep "order." The Service Department consisted of two thousand Ford employees, many of them ex-cons, former boxers, and gangsters recruited from the Michigan underworld, who intimidated, beat, and even killed suspected union men or their sympathizers, most famously at the Battle of the Overpass in 1937, when newspaper cameras captured Ford's thugs brutally beating UAW organizers outside a Dearborn factory. As poems like "Thursday Afternoons" and "Dearborn Hospitality" also suggest, though, Ford's tyranny over his workers extended beyond the factory floor to the city of Dearborn itself, where he exercised almost complete control over city officials, who in turn made it as difficult as possible (that is, illegal) for organizers to reach workers. Still, autoworkers and their union persevered, and under pressure from the U.S. government at the start of World War II, Ford eventually capitulated.

With the possible exception of the International Ladies Garment Workers or the International Workers of the World, no union published more poetry than the United Auto Workers.

King Henry the V-8th

John Paine

Oh how varied and insane
Is Henry Ford's immense domain!

At Dearborn,[1] far as eye can see,
Is mass-production industry,
Where engines, lathes, and flywheels mount
And man is held of no account.

Day by day the robots feed
The modern belt at breakneck speed;
While Greenfield Village,[2] lying near,
Embalms the ways of yesteryear.

For greater profits, Ford surmised,
Production must be organized;
But Henry doesn't have a yen
To deal with unions of his men.

---

1. Dearborn, Michigan, site of Henry Ford's sprawling River Rouge manufacturing complex. Completed in 1925, Ford and his engineers designed a "vertically integrated" plant—that is, one that could complete all the steps in the production of automobiles, from refining raw material to final assembly of the car. At its peak in the 1930s, the River Rouge factory employed more than one hundred thousand workers.

2. A reproduction of an early American village built by the nostalgic Henry Ford in the late 1920s, it contains originals or reconstructions of a steeple church, a town hall, an inn, a school, a courthouse, a general store, as well as Thomas Edison's Menlo Park workshop and the Wright brothers' cycle shop and home. The village also had a blacksmith shop, a cobbler's shop, and a tintype studio in order to illustrate early methods of industrial production.

But Ford, thank God, won't terrorize
With Pinkerton and Bergoff spies,[3]
For seeing what his own thugs do
He finds there's no occasion to.

Oh how varied and insane
Is Henry Ford's immense domain!

From United Automobile Worker, *September 1937. In the upper right and left corners of the box that contained Paine's poem there are pictures of Henry Ford's boyish face against a swastika backdrop. This graphic comparison was not unwarranted. In 1920, Henry Ford published* The International Jew, *which claimed (among other things) that Jewish bankers financed both the Communist Party and the labor unions in order to weaken industries and corporations that Jewish industrialists would then take over. Ford also encouraged and provided funds for anti-Semitic evangelists (like Gerald K. Smith and Father Charles Coughlin) and various Nazi-front organizations like the National Workers League. See also the note to "Detroit," below.*

---

3. Established in 1850, the much-reviled Pinkerton National Detective Agency supplied private security guards to factory owners, supposedly to maintain order and protect property, but in many cases to infiltrate unions, protect scabs, or, in times of strikes, to intimidate and terrorize striking workers. The Bergoff Brothers Strike Services and Labor Adjustors offered similar services, though they specialized in recruiting workers willing to cross picket lines and protecting them from striking workers as they did so. Unlike General Motors, Ford relied on his own private army. See also the note to "A Stoolie's Lament," below.

A Ford Slave

Canadian Ford Worker

To my American brothers,
And democracy lovers,
I jot down a rhyme
On company time.

To make some contribution
To industrial revolution,
And help sound the knell
Of industrial hell,

We must without fear—
Our duty is clear—
Together put a stop
To the last open shop.

End Fordham's creed
Of the stool-pigeon breed:
By organizing men
We'll stop it then—

The Fordism plan
Of exploiting man
For profit and power
From slaves by the hour.

From United Automobile Worker, *Oct. 2, 1937.*

Letting the Cat out of the Bag

Anonymous

"What did you tell that man just now?"
"I told him to hurry."
"What right do you have to tell him to hurry?"
"I pay him to hurry."
"How much do you pay him?"
"Four dollars a day."
"Where do you get the money?"
"I sell products."
"Who makes the products?"
"He does."
"How many products does he make in a day?"
"Ten dollars' worth."
"Then, instead of you paying him, he pays you $6 a day to stand around and tell him to hurry."
"Well, but I own the machines."
"How did you get the machines?"
"Sold products and bought them."
"Who made the products?"
"Shut up. He might hear you."

From United Automobile Worker, *October 1937.*

Beefsteak Blues

Tekla Roy, Pres. Flint Auxiliary

I bought a pound of meat today,
It cost me fifty cents,
I thought for once we'd have a treat
Not worrying 'bout the cents.

But when I started to prepare
The steak upon the griddle
My conscience bothered me so much
I cut it down the middle.

I put one half of it away
To save for future use.
I thought "I hope this is enough,
Oh, gee, I've got the blues."

And so it goes from day to day
Scrimp here, save there,
To make our money go around,
It surely is a care.

I'm tired of it all, aren't you?
Come on. Let's organize . . .
And fight the prices that we pay
For meat from day to day.

And if we work just like we worked
To get the union in . . .
We'll celebrate Thanksgiving Day
We'll win again, we'll win.

From United Automobile Worker, *November 13, 1937. As her signature indicates, Tekla Roy (1910–93) was president of the Flint Women's Auxiliary, the group of roughly one thousand women, many of them wives of General Motors factory workers, who organized in support of the 1936–37 Flint sit-down strike. The auxiliary, and its sister organization, the Women's Emergency Brigade, played a key, some would say decisive, role in the strike, aiding the strikers in countless ways and battling police when they tried to retake the factory. Roy also taught public speaking and labor history to the wives of Flint workers.*

To Alfred P. Sloan

Clayton Fountain

Alf,[1] old kid, forgive our liberty
In talking to you so familiarly;
It's pretty hard for workers to respect
A boss so stubborn that he can't direct—
If not a bonus—then at least some thanks
To those who put his millions in the banks.

Four days a week is one swell Christmas gift
To those who can't begin to practice thrift,
Because you have refused to raise the pay
That barely lets us live from day to day—
Although the fact remains: 'Twas we who made
All of the dividends so lately paid.[2]

Apparently you think that laying off
The union boys—while your stool pigeons scoff
And curse the union[3]—will arouse disgust
And undermine the workers' faith and trust
In their own union's power to preserve
Security and gain what they deserve.

We guess that's one on you, old top. You see,
We're not the dumbbells that we used to be:
Keep your damn bonuses; we're going to fight
With all our strength for what we think is right.
None of your schemes can separate
Us from the UAWA.

---

1. Alfred P. Sloan was president and CEO of General Motors.
2. Unlike other car manufacturers, General Motors continued to turn a profit throughout the Depression, returning roughly 18 percent on capital investment over an eighteen-year period that included the worst years of the early 1930s.
3. See note to "A Stoolie's Lament," below.

From United Auto Worker, *December 18, 1937. Clayton Fountain (1909–93) was born, according to his autobiography, "in a log cabin on the Lake Michigan shore of the Upper Peninsula of Michigan." After wandering the country and holding a variety of odd jobs, Clayton moved to Detroit in 1928 and found work in various auto-manufacturing plants—Packard, Briggs, Chevrolet, ultimately General Motors. During the Depression, he was laid off, sold vacuum cleaners door to door, and was a laborer on local public works projects. In 1936, Fountain, back in the auto industry, joined the Communist Party and the UAW. In addition to being elected to several official posts in the UAW—including educational director of Local 285— Fountain was also an editor for the* United Auto Worker, *the newspaper of the union. Before World War II, Fountain broke with the Communist Party, and in 1949 he published a fascinating prounion, anti-Communist memoir entitled* Union Guy.

What We Want
George F. Young

A six-hour day,
A five-day week,
With no less pay
Is what we seek.

From United Automobile Worker, *December 18, 1937. The poem was accompanied by the following note from the author: "To the Editor: Here is a little poem which I believe tells the truth about that which is wanted by all workers. It should be printed on the front page of every labor newspaper in this country and also should be learned by all the workers."*

A Stoolie's Lament
Murray Roth, Local 262, Detroit

Says Slim-de rat: It knocks me flat
　　Cause people think I'm foolin'
Me woik is art, it breaks me heart
　　To have 'em call it stoolin![1]

---

1. Unlike Henry Ford, who relied on his in-house Service Department and his own paid labor spies, General Motors preferred outside detective agencies, including the infamous Pinkertons, all of which came to light as a result of the La Follette Committee hearings in 1936. That year, Congress convened the committee to investigate the tactics of antiunion employers— espionage, private detectives, munitioning, strikebreaking—on the grounds that such actions deprived workers of their civil rights. In particular, the La Follette Committee singled out General Motors for its "truly magnificent" commitment to labor espionage. Between January 1934 and July 1936, the committee discovered, GM paid private detective agencies like the Pinkertons the scarcely imaginable sum of just under a million dollars for its labor

De CIO has made it so
    Me job is gittin' fearful,
I has to stoop and sneak and snoop
    To git me dirty earful.

I've often thought, if I get caught
    And now that I'm a goner.
I'll give de boss de double cross,
    Upon me word of honor.

Now folks can see dat blokes like me
    Has got to use discretion,
In times like dese, I earns my cheese
    De party of my profession.

From United Automobile Worker, *December 18, 1937.*

---

espionage services, observing that GM had built "the most colossal supersystem of spies yet devised in any American corporation." As a result of this near-total surveillance, workers in places like Flint suspected almost everyone of spying for the company and consequently feared expressing any interest in unions lest they lose their jobs.

The House That Jack Built

Elizabeth England

This is the house that Jack built,
This is the dream
That grows in the house that Jack built;

These are the rats
Despoiling the dream
That grows in the house that Jack built.

What is the House That Jack Built?

America's the house that Jack built.

    Who is Jack

Jack is the worker
Who breaks the trail

And lays the road;
Who hews the forest
And mines the oar;
Who grows the grain
And weaves the cloth;
That fashions the dream
That grows in the house that Jack built.

What is the Dream?

This is the dream,
Now withered and sterile,
This is the dream:
To shelter the weak
And strengthen the strong;
To spread the table
And open the door;
To bring in the light
And give Tomorrow
To all who work in the house that Jack built.

This is the dream
Now withered and sterile;
This is the dream
Gnawed by rats
That infest the house that Jack built.

Who Are the Rats?

These are the rats:
Millowner—banker—
Landlord—boss—
Greedy and ruthless,
Armed with force;

These are the rats,
Fattened on greed,
Who steal the trail
And ravage the forest;
Who waste the ore
And corner the grain;

Who defile the cloth
That fashions the dream
That grows in the house that Jack built.

How Can Jack Be Rid of Rats?

This is the way:
The only way
Unite the Jack
Who breaks the trail
With the Jack
Who lays the road;
Unite the Jack
Who hews the forest
With the Jack
Who mines the ore;
Unite the Jack
Who grows the grain
With the Jack
Who weaves the cloth.

For united the Jacks
Can build a trap;
Can catch the rats
That spoil the dream
That grows in the house that Jack built;
United the Jacks—
Rid of the rats—
Can rebuild the house
Make real the dream,
Spread the table,
Open the door;
Bring in the light
And give Tomorrow,
To all who work in the house that Jack built.

From United Automobile Worker, *December 25, 1937. The poem borrows the title and form of one of the familiar Mother Goose nursery rhymes.*

Thursday Afternoons

George A. Medalis

You can't pass your papers here, boys
    An ordinance (they say)
A nuisance, an obstruction
    (Men may be led astray!)[1]

So put them in the wagon, boys
    Escort them to a cell
They must be agitators
    (Bennet[2] said "give 'em hell!")

Yes, burn that pile of papers, boys
    They'll pass no more today
The mayor gave those orders
    (Ford tells him what to say!)

From United Automobile Worker, *January 1, 1938.*

---

1. In 1937, the Dearborn City Council passed an ordinance that prohibited leafleting in "congested areas" of the city, including the "congested" area outside the River Rouge factory. The ordinance was just one of the ways Ford used his control over local government and police to intimidate would-be organizers and to impede any attempt to organize Ford workers.
2. Harry Bennett (Medalis spells it "Bennet" in the poem), head of Ford's notorious Service Department. See note to "Ford Sunday Evening Hour" for Bennett's role in the 1932 Ford Hunger March.

As Uncle Henry Would Have Us Pray

Francis Reardon, Chassis Dept.

Mr. Ford is my master, I am in want,
He maketh me to lie down on park bench
He locketh me out of his factory
He disturbeth my soul
He leadeth me in the path of destruction
For my union's sake.

Yea, though I walk through the valley of destruction
I anticipate no recovery.
For he is with me
He prepareth a reduction in my salary
And in the presence of my enemies
He annointeth my income with thugs,
And my expenses runneth over
Surely unemployment and poverty
Will follow me all the days of my life.
And I shall dwell in a mortgaged house forever.

From United Automobile Worker, *January 16, 1938. The poem adapts the 23rd Psalm, which begins "The Lord is my shepherd; I shall not want."*

Dearborn Hospitality

Murray Roth, Local 262

I'm a convict doing time
For a very vicious crime.
Yes—they caught me in Henry's foreign land!
Though they shivered in their pants,
Fifty coppers took a chance
As they seized the paper weapons in my hand.[1]

After much ado and fuss,
In the mayor's special bus
I was driven to a hoosegow[2] down the street
When I tried to pay my fare
To the man who drove me there,
I was told that it was Mayor Carey's[3] treat.

---

1. See note to "Thursday Afternoons," above, for the City of Dearborn's ordinances against leafleting.
2. "Hoosegow" is slang for a jail or guardhouse. It is a phonetic spelling of the Spanish word *juzgar*, "to judge."
3. John L. Carey, mayor of Dearborn, Michigan, 1936–42.

I was taken to my doom
In an overcrowded room . . .
To a cell where many others shared my sin.
As they placed me in this cell
Every man began to yell . . .
"Show your union card or we won't let you in!"

I don't blame the boys in blue
For the dirty work they do.
They must do their job the same as you or I.
When they free me from this pen
I'll be coming back again,
For I love this Dearborn hospitality.

From United Automobile Worker, *February 12, 1938.*

I am the picket

Ralph H. Marlatt

I am the picket;
The army marched against me in '77,[1]

I was beaten at Homestead in '93,[2]
I was shot at Pullman,[3]
Arrested at Lawrence;[4]
They burned my kids at Ludlow

---

1. In 1877, railroad workers conducted the first national strike in U.S. history, which was finally broken by a combination of federal and state troops, leading to the death of several dozen striking workers and citizens.
2. The 1892 Homestead, Pennsylvania, steel strike. See note to "Here Goes Steel!" in the United Steel Workers section.
3. In 1894, striking Pullman Palace Car Company workers, led by a young Eugene Debs, precipitated a national railroad strike, which, like the 1877 strike, was broken by a combination of federal and state troops, leaving thirteen dead and fifty wounded. Debs would eventually be imprisoned for his role in the strike.
4. In 1912, twenty thousand textile workers, led by the IWW, won a sixty-day strike, though the leaders of that strike, Arturo Giovannitti and Joseph Ettor, were both imprisoned on trumped-up murder charges.

To help pile up Rockefeller dimes.[5]
They called me a Bolshevik in '19[6]
Because I asked for an eight-hour day,
They murdered me in Chicago in '37,[7]
Beat and slugged and gassed me in Detroit,[8] Akron,[9]
I am the picket,
In the midst of misery,
In the face of injustice.
With the dead past and the dying present
I march
All hell can't beat me down,
I am the picket.

From United Automobile Worker, *June 18, 1938.*

---

5. In 1913, Ludlow, Colorado, miners struck John D. Rockefeller's Colorado Fuel and Iron Company; after workers and their families were evicted from their company-owned homes, they set up a tent camp, which the state militia attacked and set fire to, killing fourteen people, including eleven children. Later, during his philanthropist phase, Rockefeller would grow famous for handing out dimes to the public.
6. In 1919, hundreds of thousands of workers in almost every major industry went on strike. Coming on the heels of the Russian Revolution, the national strikes contributed to the nation's first red scare.
7. In what was subsequently called the Memorial Day Massacre, police shot ten unarmed strikers outside Republic Steel in Chicago.
8. The Ford Hunger March. See note to "Ford Sunday Evening Hour," below.
9. In 1937, rubber workers conducted the first sit-down strike at the Firestone tire plant, during which police and private guards attacked pickets.

Detroit

Ralph H. Marlatt

Detroit,
The auto capital of the world.
Idle factories, hunger lines,

And a birthday party for the king.[1]

I visited the morgue
And saw a tray full of babies.
They found them in alleys and ash-cans,
The man said, "we get lots of them,
The welfare sends a lot too,
Their people are too poor to bury them."

I sat in an office,
Politicians came in to talk;
The secretary was late for dinner,
He said, "we'll lick the unions.
We don't need a union in this town,
Reserve me a ticket for the Cruise."

I talked to a man,
Worked twenty-one years in one place,
Never could get anything ahead
Too many short seasons, lay-offs,
He said, "I'm too old now, I'm through,
Young men can work faster."

Detroit,
The auto capital of the world.
Idle factories, hunger lines,
And a birthday party for the king.

From United Automobile Worker, *July 16, 1938.*

1. On July 30, 1938, fifteen hundred prominent Detroit citizens gathered to celebrate Henry Ford's seventy-fifth birthday. The dinner achieved notoriety when, in recognition of Ford's substantial financial support for Adolph Hitler's nationalist and anti-Semitic movements in Munich in the 1920s and his continued support in the 1930s, a representative of Hitler's Nazi Germany presented Ford with the Grand Cross of the German Eagle, the Nazi decoration for distinguished foreigners.

Have you ever worked on a line puttin' out five thousand bodies a day?

Ralph H. Marlatt

Have you ever worked on a line puttin' out five thousand bodies a day?
Then, brother, you ain't ever been to hell;
The bell rings and the line starts,
Bend, lift, hammer, screw,
No stopping now 'til noon, or 'til you drop,
Bend, lift, hammer, screw,
And the sweat pouring into your eyes and mouth
'Til your lips are puffed with the salt of it,
Your dripping hair hangs in your eyes
And you can't take time to push it back,
And your belly turns over at the smell of garlic,
Turns sick at the stench of human bodies,
Turns sick at guys spittin' tobacco juice and blood,
Bend, lift, hammer, screw,
Get production, the eternal cry,
Your back feels like it's about to bust
And you can't straighten up or stretch,
And the line keeps pushin' bodies at you,
And there ain't no way you can hold 'em back,
Bend, lift, hammer, screw,
Oh, Christ, where is that bell,
Bend, lift, hammer, screw,
Four hours of it and then fifteen minutes to eat,
Bolt a hunk of bread and at it again,
Bend, lift, hammer, screw;
Have you ever worked on a line puttin' out five thousand bodies a day?
Then, brother, you ain't ever been to hell.

From United Automobile Worker, *October 8, 1938.*

We are the auto workers

Ralph H. Marlatt

We are the auto workers,
A million wheels turning,
In the great machine of life,
Toilers on the line,
Keepers of the belt,
Putting the world on wheels.

I come from the deep south,
Where the smell of magnolias
Is like a breath of heaven
And the soft whisper of night
Is the wind in the palms;
I work on the motor line
And I smell of grease and sweat.

I come from the far east,
A land of mythical beauty,
My people are of the ages,
Their wisdom is found in ancient script
And poems carved in stone;
I file the edges of bearing caps
And I think of nothing as I race the belt.

I come from the mountains of the west,
The wide-open spaces where there is room to breathe,
Where all the outdoors is given to man to own,
To sleep but under the stars,
Or ride for hours in the clean, sweet air;
I work in the sand-blast,
My lungs are caked with dust and I choke and cough.

I come from the frozen north,
Where the wind is like a keen knife,
Where men are spurred on by the challenge of nature,
Where there is freshness that keeps you awake

And every fibre in you responds to life;
I work in the rolling mill
It is hot, and my body aches and I am weary.

We are the auto workers.
A million wheels turning
In the great machine of life,
From the ends of the earth we are gathered
To become keepers of the belt,
Putting the world on wheels.

From United Automobile Worker, *March 25, 1939.*

The people
Anonymous

The people,
Toiling to build a nation:
Across the western plains
Mile after mile stretch wheat fields,
And railroad workers carry the grain to Minneapolis
To be ground into flour, tons of it
And millions of Americans are hungry;
In Gary they make steel,
And automobiles in Detroit,
In the southeast miners are coughing their lungs out
To dig coal for the nation,
And millions of Americans are without heat;
In New York and along the Atlantic Coast,
Toilers weave cloth, make suits and dresses,
Fashion shoes and boots,
And millions of Americans are without clothing;
The people
Toiling to build a nation,
For what?

From United Automobile Worker, *November 26, 1938.*

Fordism
Tobie

A quicker step, a bit more sweat,
I may make my production yet.
A bit more speed (Ford Motor creed),
A thousand more is all I need.
A slip, a miss, I hear a hiss,
The boss behind has noticed this.
An hour to go, I must be slow,
A pair of eyes has told me so.
The day is done; I fail by one.
"Take three days off, you son-of-gun!"

From United Automobile Worker, *April 29, 1939.*

Ford Sunday Evening Hour
Anonymous

Between dark and daylight on Sunday,
When the night is beginning to lower,
Comes a wonderful radio program,
The Ford Sunday Evening Hour.[1]

I hear from my seat in the corner
The music so soft and so sweet,
The voice of a wonderful tenor
And life seems full and complete.

1. This line, as well as the poem's title, refers to the Ford-sponsored radio program of the same name, which broadcast classical music out of Dearborn, Michigan, to an enormous national (as well as local) audience. Interspersed with the music, *The Ford Sunday Evening Hour* featured the host of the program, W. J. Cameron, giving "talks" on a range of subjects—patriotism, holidays, America—and, just as frequently, on the "so-called" labor and social problems of the 1930s. Many of the latter talks consisted of homespun briefs against the Roosevelt administration and its New Deal reforms. Like Ford, Cameron objected to the New Deal on the grounds that it supposedly restrained the beneficent ambitions of management and business, therefore harming civilization itself.

Then we listen to Ford's Mr. Cameron
And the guest star who prostitutes art,
Who is paid to make beautiful music
And buy Henry's way to our heart.

But in spite of the wonderful music
And in spite of the soft spoken lies,
I know they are plotting and planning
To take me by surprise.

They fairly engulf me with music,
My senses they try to o'erpower,
And they try to ruin my judgment
With their wonderful symphony hour.

Then a sudden hush of the music
And life seems full and complete—
Then Cameron steps up to the mouthpiece
And over the air he bleats.

He condemns the unions and labor,
And when he rants no more
A beautiful symphony concert
Has been spoiled by an arrogant bore.

But the strains of the music return them
And the peace and contentment steal back,
But it seems that something is missing,
There is something which life seems to lack.

And somehow from out of the music
Come visions of days that are past,
And my peace and contentment all leave me,
It seems that they just cannot last.

Still I settle down in my armchair,
But I remember a day long ago
When Henry Ford's plant wasn't running
And the workers were out in the snow.

So they decided to go out to Dearborn,
And try to see Henry Ford,
To see if they couldn't find some way
To pay for their bed and their board.

But all of you know the story
How he met them with tear gas and guns
And workers were beaten and tear-gassed
By Bennett's stool pigeons and thugs.[2]

And next day it came out in the papers
How a bunch of radical Reds
Had planned to take over the factory
And murder the Fords in their beds.

Now the music dies out in the distance,
They announce a lovely old hymn,
Giving all glory to God
And singing their praises to Him.

But I wonder if those up in Heaven
Ever look down from above
And see guns, tear-gas and nightsticks,
A symbol of Ford's brand of love?

Do you think, Henry Ford, you exploiter
You can buy with this kind of stuff
The thanks and goodwill of thousands
Who haven't nearly enough?

---

2. The speaker is recalling the Ford Hunger March, which remains one of the signal events of the Depression years. By August 1931, the Ford Motor Company had laid off three out of every four of its 128,000 workers. On March 7, 1932, three thousand protestors—including many unemployed Ford workers organized by the Communist-led Auto Workers Union—marched from the outskirts of Detroit to the River Rouge plant in Dearborn demanding jobs for laid-off Ford workers, a slowdown of the company's assembly line, and a halt to evictions of ex-Ford workers from company housing. As the marchers neared the plant, the Dearborn police threatened to arrest them if they did not turn back and, when the marchers did not in fact disperse, fired tear gas at them. The marchers responded by throwing rocks and lumps of frozen dirt, and one protester knocked the chief of Ford's private army, Harry Bennett, unconscious. In response to that barrage, a battery of city police and company guards rushed from the Ford plant gates and opened point-blank fire on the crowd, killing four workers and wounding more than sixty.

If you do, you're fooled plenty
For you are seeing the dawn of a day
When the workers will be educated,
For the CIO's here to stay.

So you might as well keep your music
And shut old Cameron's yap,
For while we enjoy your music
We haven't time for your crap.

And although I hear your good music
I remember that day long ago—
So keep all your love and your music,
Just give us the CIO.

So we'll stick in the union forever
Yes, forever and a day,
Till the power of Ford has vanished
And the workers have gained a new day.

From United Automobile Worker, *May 13, 1939.*

pressure

Poll

come on there cutter . . .
set the job up . . .
fix it tight . . .
use the fan . . .
let it blow full cold . . .
here's castor oil . . .
and grease
to help the bearings
best it can . . .
then push it . . .
push it . . .

push it . . .
freeze the machine solid . . .
if you must . . .
but get the job out . . .
fast . . .
double quick . . .
5000 men stand waiting . . .
5000 hours a'wasting . . .
overhead
mounting . . .
mounting . . .
mounting . . .
come on there cutter . . .
let the shavings fly . . .
cut the steel . . .
16th by 16th . . .
push the motor . . .
grease the bearings . . .
let the fan blow . . .
push it . . .
push it . . .
for gods sake cutter . . .
get the job out . . .

From United Automobile Worker, *May 13, 1939.*

"you work tomorrow"

Poll

my shift
checks in at eight . . .

this time
the checkers saying . . .
"no more work
unless notified" . . .

that's a way
to begin a day . . .
with the future stretching
out in emptiness . . .
and your wife's face
growing troubled . . .
your children
going silent
before you . . .
and only the mailman's coming
to mark off the days
until the recall comes . . .

nine
ten
eleven o'clock . . .

and the work on your machine
fades in the fog of your desire
for that tap on the shoulder
your super will give you
if
you work tomorrow . . .

and you can't get your job right
and you crack your foot
with a tool at the crib . . .
because your hands won't hold . . .

noon . . .
check out for lunch . . .
with your food all hard
and your coffee all dry in your throat . . .

check in . . .
with the checker still saying . . .
"no more work
unless notified" . . .

one
two
three o'clock . . .

there's no more use
trying to work . . .
just watch the super . . .
up the aisles and down . . .
but he never stops . . .
and you begin to wonder
at the use of it all . . .

let your children want . . .
let your wife go mad with worrying . . .
let the landlord wave writs in your face . . .

god for the chance
at warring in spain . . .
let's go to china
and fight the japs . . .[1]
let's do anything
but wait
wait
wait . . .
for the super
to tap you on the shoulder
and say the words . . .
"you work tomorrow"
just that
"you work tomorrow" . . .

and here he is again
and you want to turn
and laugh in his face . . .
only he's tapping you on the shoulder

---

1. On Spain, see note to "Madrid" in the Industrial Workers of the World section. In September 1931, Japan invaded Manchuria, followed in July 1937 by an all-out war on mainland China. Shortly thereafter, Japanese troops began to indiscriminately slaughter hundreds of thousands of Chinese citizens, especially in the city of Nanking.

and leaning over
to say
"you work tomorrow" . . .

and your knees are trembling . . .
and there's sweat all over you . . .
and you want to puke your guts out . . .

but the whistle blows . . .
and you turn . . .
and there's joe . . .
packing his tools in his case . . .
and hans . . .
and almost every other man . . .
in the goddam place . . .

what should it matter to you . . .
you've got your notice . . .
but pull your hat
down over your face . . .
and grab your lunch box . . .
and hurry the hell
out of the place . . .

to breathe the open air
and look up at all the stacks . . .
smoking . . .
and the factory stretching out
in all directions . . .

and the men
pouring out of all the doors . . .
with their tool boxes
under their arms . . .

but you . . .
you work tomorrow . . .

From United Automobile Worker, *May 20, 1939.*

United Electrical, Radio, and Machine Workers of America

The United Electrical, Radio, and Machine Workers of America started from a union of radio workers at a Philadelphia Philco plant in 1933. After repeated jurisdictional disputes with the AFL and the rival International Brotherhood of Electrical Workers, in 1936 the UE affiliated with the CIO and in 1937 launched a major organizing drive, increasing fourfold—to 120,000—its membership of workers who built radios and other electrical appliances for companies like General Electric and Westinghouse.

For its relatively late start, the UE published a good deal of poetry, too, much of it from the pen of Walter Mugford, a toolmaker, organizer, and frequent contributor to the *UE News* who eventually earned the title "Poet Laureate of the UE." Two of his poems, "The Five-Point Plan" and "Help!" express workers' frustration with the various and little understood incentive schemes—"piecework" by another name—that tied wages to productivity. Another Mugford poem, "Never Again," is one of a number of antiwar poems that appeared in the labor press prior to Pearl Harbor. Though they hated Hitler's Fascism and its suppression of unions, many workers opposed U.S. entry into World War II, fearing that it would repeat the war-profiteering and pointless violence of World War I, distract from the problems of unemployment and housing at home, and roll back what gains workers had achieved in the second half of the 1930s. Mugford also recruited poets for the *UE News,* including Jack McGowan, whose "A Helper's Prayer" is a reflection on the apprenticeship system among skilled tool-and-die makers. Finally, Floyd C. Bates's "Lament of a Michigander" is a send-up of Luren D. Dickinson, Michigan's somewhat comically pious governor.

The Five-Point Plan

Walter Mugford, Local 422

In Westinghouse, so help me, Bob
Five people grade me on my job.
If those five folk could all agree
My life might much more simpler be.
But if with one my face won't fit,
The jury will always be split
And then, to put it mild and brief,
My life may be all toil and grief.

My foreman says my work's O.K.,
And I deserve a raise in pay.
But as my features start to glow,
Adds, "Damn it all—your grade is low!"
And should I venture to ask why,
He fixes me with frosty eye.
"I grade you well," he says, "And so
"To your group leader you must go."

That gentleman asserts that I
With him am rated aces high.
Inspector and rate-setting man
Both swear my work they never pan.
And so that young production clerk
Is doing all the dirty work!
In plain disgust I give it up,
And hie me home to sleep and sup.
Since I can't live on plain soft soap,
The UE is my only hope.

From UE News, May 13, 1939. Walter Mugford (likely 1889–1965) was a UE organizer in New Jersey, Illinois, Massachusetts, Vermont, and, in the mid-1940s, Pennsylvania. The UE archive housed at the University of Pittsburgh contains correspondence from Mugford as well as several unpublished poems. "The Five-Point Plan" was accompanied by the following note from the author: "The 'grading' system used in the Westinghouse Meter Division in Newark is a puzzle to everyone concerned. Even the members of the 'Grading Committees,' when questioned, scratch their heads and say 'It's simple,' and let it go at that."

Help!

Walter Mugford

I've had puzzles in geometry
    And algebra and such,
Problems in trigonometry
    That have bewildered me much.

And Chinese puzzles I have solved
    As easy as can be,
Yet may I be from blame absolved,
    That "Grading Plan" beats me.

Now Mary Blank worked hard all day
    (As all admit she should),
For Mary figured in this way
    Her "grading" would be good.

But one day Mary had a date,
    And so she watched the clock;
Too soon she reached the factory gate—
    Her "grading" was in hock.

Then Jimmy Umph: A job spoiled he;
    And came in late, what's more.
Jim feared that he disgraced would be
    With "low grade" on that score.

But Brothers, judge of our surprise
    When "grading" time came round—
For scarce could we believe our eyes,
    Jimmy Number One was found!

May hap 'tis cause I'm growing old
    This throws me for a loss,
With silver threads among the gold
    My brain's not what it was.

From UE News, *1939.*

Lament of a Michigander

Floyd C. Bates, UE Local 113

Oh hearken ye Michigan People
To the tale of an Earthly Clod;
The one little, lonely Mortal
Who can boast of a pipeline to God.

'Tis the Ruler of Michigan's People
This one of whom I would relate,
He pipelines his prayers to Jehovah
To advise him on matters of State.

Is this a bad bill? Shall I veto?
Is this a good bill to be signed?
He claims he is answered by pipeline
From the Holy One's Eternal Mind.

I know there are some of his subjects
Who more than a little suspect,
The Devil is tapping the pipeline
And garbling the answers he gets.

For he okays bad bills with excuses,
And discards the good ones with Prayer,
'Tho it may be advised by the pipeline
It's beginning to get in our hair.

He promised to balance the budget,
And now we have found to our grief,
His method is cutting the school fund
And lower the poor man's relief.

He proposes to banish (hard likker),
With the W.C.T.U.[1]
He worries about the girls' morals,
As men of his age often do.

---

1. Women's Christian Temperance Union, a prohibitionist group founded in 1873 and active throughout the first decades of the twentieth century.

The fate that's confronting our daughters
Is marriage with bare cupboard shelves.
If he'll loosen up on the welfare
They'll care for their morals themselves.

We hope he won't wax egotistic
Trying too many burdens to bear,
Or try to advise the Almighty
On balancing budgets up there.

If the Heavenly budget were balanced
On advice of the Doddering Clown,
There'd be hungry, illiterate Angels
Without even a Robe or a Crown.

We recall that he tried to play milkmaid,
And fell off that three-legged stool,
We doubt 'twas advised by the pipeline
We surmise 'twas the act of a fool.

We just can't imagine a Christian
Going into his closet to Pray,
Surrounded by newspaper cameras,
His piety thus to display.[2]

Think how happy it makes crippled children,
Whom he cut off from hospital care,
Just to know that their Ruler is Pious
And strongly addicted to Prayer.

It may be the Ruler is hoping
Extra Stars in his crown there will be,
If he literally follows the order,
"Let the little ones come unto Me!"

Now we'd like to point out to the Ruler
That he's making a little mistake,
For when the Lord Jesus said, "Let them"
He certainly didn't mean, "MAKE."

---

2. The stool incident and prayer closet are from popular newspaper accounts of Dickinson, who made much of his simple, unpretentious farm and farmhouse in Eaton County, Michigan.

Our Ruler emphatically tells us
That prayers are still answered today,
And if this be true then I say to you
Oh people of Michigan PRAY.

Drop right down on your prayer bones
And pray with a fervent seal,
Oh pray for the sake of your native State
Oh pray for her people's weal.

Let this be the prayer that you utter,
"Oh Lord, send this pious old fraud
An urgently voiced invitation
To SHIN UP THE PIPELINE TO GOD."

From UE News, August 26, 1939. Luren D. Dickinson was first lieutenant governor of Michigan, then governor of that state from 1939 to 1940 after the elected governor, Frank Fitzgerald, died in office. Dickinson once told a Sunday school class, "What Paul really did was get on a pipeline to God. You can do the same thing. I did it many years ago."

"Never Again"

Walter Mugford

"A war to end war" fought in vain!
Europe is drenched in blood again.
Again the flames of passion fan
Man's inhumanity to man.
And bomb and bullet, mine and shell,
Turn fairest fields to foulest hell.
Starvation, sorrow, sin and shame
Are sown anew in glory's name.
While brave men die and women weep,
That statesmen may their prestige keep,
And children raised in dark despair
Find ruthless ruin everywhere.

Four years fought I for England's fame,[1]
Thinking the Kaiser was to blame.
Dreaming poor fool, the blood of me
Was shed to spare democracy.
For what fought we? A nation's pride?
Why have those brave boys fought and died?
Through dripping bayonets, mud, and lice,
God, what a turmoil: What a price
In twisted bodies, broken lives.
In ruined homes, demented wives.
Now must their sons face anew
The horrors that their fathers knew?
And must their daughters weep in vain
For husbands, brothers, sweethearts slain?
Perish the thought! Let every man
Lift loud his voice while yet he can.
Let every woman, every child,
Refuse this time to be beguiled
By those whose greedy minds well know
Red rain will make their profits grow.
Let labor learn such wars are vain.
Then may we live in peace again.

From UE News, *October 16, 1939.*

---

1. Since the United States did not enter World War I until 1917, and the war concluded in 1918, this line may seem confusing. There are several possible explanations. Mugford may be British, having fought in World War I from the start, and subsequently immigrated to America; he may be one of the rare Americans who enlisted in the British army at the start of the war in 1914; or, perhaps most likely, he is adopting the persona of a British soldier.

Real Americans

Al Rimer, Local 502, St. Mary's, Pa.

The public, it appears, is to prone to think
    That a good union man is a tough, lawless gink—
A guy who tries constantly to holdup his boss
    And throw innocent stockholders for a hard, costly loss.

Thus before organization was thought of in town
    Our reputations were high but our wages were down,
But now we've signed with the strong CIO
    We get few invitations but we do get more dough.

And dough is what counts, the old reliable jack,
    When you call at a store to buy things that you lack.
Plainly then we've saved business from slow strangulation
    By forcing more coin into circulation.

From UE News, *1941.*

A Helper's Prayer

Jack McGowan

Oh, for a hacksaw and hammer,
A rule, some pipe and a wrench;
    And a ratchet and die
    With an oil can nigh
Plus a vise on an ironbound bench;
Yes a vise on an ironbound bench.

Oh, and give me a print to read;
A layout to guide me thru;
    I'll work it out
    With never a doubt;
And I'll put the pipe up too;
Yes I'll put the pipe up too.

Oh, I'm sick of walking behind
A fitter with all the load;
 I'm just a slave
 For an early grave
And my legs are getting bowed;
Yes my legs *are* getting bowed.

Oh, and I want some tools, by gosh
And a helper to growl and swear;
 I'm gonna be tough
 And I'll treat him rough
Till he learns this helper's prayer;
Yes, till he learns this helper's prayer.

From UE News, *December 1, 1941. The poem was accompanied by the following note from the editor: "Pittsfield, Mass., December 1—Walter Mugford isn't only a poet himself—he's also a finder of other poets. This week, the UE bard, who's organizing when he isn't poetizing, rhymes out the news of discovery of another versifier in the ranks of UE Local 255. Here's Poet-Scout Mugford's report." Walter Mugford's short, unremarkable poem, "Introducing Another Bard," follows the editor's note.*

United Mine Workers of America

The United Mine Workers played prominent roles—perhaps the prominent role—in both the history of labor unions in the late nineteenth and early twentieth centuries and the history of labor song and poetry in that period. Like many unions, the United Mine Workers' origins date back to the Great Uprising of the 1880s and 1890s, and at least in the coal fields of western Pennsylvania, Ohio, Indiana, and Illinois, miners experienced considerable success in their attempts to organize the competitive and exploitative coal industry. By the turn of the century, more than 250,000 miners belonged to the UMWA, and they had done much to correct the traditional abuses in wages and working conditions that had characterized work in the mines. (Outside of those Midwestern areas, however, miners stood little chance of organizing given the rabidly antiunion mine owners and the state militias and private police forces those owners could command.)

When World War I ended, though, the demand for coal fell off, mechanization threw many miners out of work, and, in an effort to reduce labor costs, mine owners across the country launched an open-shop movement that decimated the union. Like the International Ladies Garment Workers Union, the United Mine Workers took advantage of the National Industrial Recovery Act and its promise of union recognition and collective bargaining for all workers by launching a major organizing campaign; by the end of 1933, the union had organized over 90 percent of the coal mines in the country. More than any other union, too, the United Mine Workers, under the leadership of the ruthless but shrewd John L. Lewis, helped launch the Committee of Industrial Organization in 1935, breaking with the American Federation of Labor and providing much-needed funds and organizers that would, within a few years, assist in the unionization of nearly four million new workers in the auto, steel, rubber, meatpacking, and electrical equipment industries.

In addition to their role in the history of industrial unionism, though, miners also belong at the center of the history of labor song and poetry. Beginning in the mid-1920s, and with United Mine Worker funding and support, the folklorist George Korson spent a lifetime documenting what he called the "amazing vogue" "balladry attained . . . among the anthracite mine workers" in the nineteenth and early twentieth centuries. (Indeed, much of Korson's work originally appeared in the *United Mine Workers Journal,* though he later gathered it into three collections, *Songs and Ballads of the Anthracite Miners* [1927], *Minstrels of the Mine Patch* [1938], and *Coal Dust on the Fiddle* [1943].) As detailed in the introduction to this anthology, Korson regretted the effect that modernity—popular education, the newspaper, the automobile, the movies, and the radio—had on miners' folklore, but his regret seems to have been exaggerated since miners continued to publish poetry in the *United Mine Workers Journal* throughout the 1930s. In addition, a vast number of displaced and unemployed miners migrated to northern and Midwestern industrial cities, bringing their tradition of industrial unionism and labor balladry with them.

The poems that followed all appeared in the *United Mine Workers Journal.* Some, like "Children of the Mine" and "Union Stew," appeared on the *Journal's* "A Page for Women." (That page also frequently reprinted the work of canonical poets like Alfred Tennyson and William Wordsworth.) Most of the other poems come from two minianthologies of dozens or more poems that appeared in the *Journal* in the second half of the 1930s. Many poems—like "Verses from West Virginia," "Union Stew," "Machinery vs. Men," and "The Miner"—resemble others in this collection, especially, in the case of "The Miner," the "hell poems" that recur throughout labor poetry. But other poems, like "Children of the Mine," "The Fatal Gilberton Mine," and "When Daddy Gets a Raise," are best read in the tradition of the ballad, where sentimentalism is a deliberately sought-for effect and not necessarily a result of amateurish sincerity. Still other poems, like "Pick Coal Rhythm" and "The Coal-Miner's Blues," as their titles indicate, also belong in the tradition of miners' songs and ballads, though their use of dialect and humor (respectively) place them more squarely in a blues tradition.

Children of the Mine

Joseph Poggianni

Along the road of the grim mining town
    Plod the children to school in silent way,
Plod with the fragile bodies leaning down
    And sullen eyes, as stricken by dismay;
While their minds turn to the unhappy home,
    Once a live place to sing and laugh and roam.

Father is idle, discarded and pushed aside
    By steel monsters who dig and load the coal;
Mother—poor mother—struggles hard to provide
    The essential things out of scanty dole,
And her heart bleeds in agonizing mood
    Over the future of the tender brood.

Innocent victims of a cruel fate,
    Shall they grow cursing the day they saw light?
Shall they strive in a field of spite and hate
    To lose and die in unequal fight?
O Lord of mercy, with Thy love divine
    Bless and assist the children of the mine!

From United Mine Workers Journal, *February 15, 1935.*

Verses from West Virginia

Anonymous (From Mingo County)

Just a verse from West Virginia,
    From the Mingo County hills,
Along the banks of old Tug Ruver,
    Where the engine whistle shrills.

Where we see the coal trains speeding,
    From the stack the black smoke roll,
And we know the boiler's steaming
    For it's burning union coal.

And the whole train crew is happy,
  As they speed along their way,
For the boiler's steaming nicely
  And there will be no delay.

As the fireman hollers "green board!"
  When the engine rounds the turn,
The safety valve is popping—
  It's the union coal they burn.

It's clean coal the engine's burning,
  The crew knows it won't be late,
For the miners have a contract
  And no more they're loading slate.[1]

They have scales at all the tipples,
  And they closely watch the beam,
For it's plain in the contract
  That they've got to load it clean.

Now every one is happy,
  As they watch the trains each day,
For they know the coal their hauling
  Brings the miners better pay.

And they work just seven hours,
  And to you they all will say,
We can better feed our families
  By the union contract way.

Now they'll never shirk their duty,
  As to being union men,
And they'll stand by John L. Lewis
  And Van Bittner to the end.[2]

From United Mine Workers Journal, *April 1, 1937.*

---

1. By "loading slate," a miner could artificially increase the weight of mined coal and thus his wages.
2. John L. Lewis, president of the UMWA from 1920 to 1960. Van A. Bittner, officer in the UMWA and later head of the Packinghouse Workers Organizing Committee.

Pick Coal Rhythm

Lou Barrelle and Andy Lucas

If you look for job, I tell you true,
The coal mine, he no place for you;
If you listen while I tell,
He some place just like hell.

The coal, he dirty, bottom wet,
To dig him under make you sweat,
Bore through boney, sulphur—all,
Shoot five times and he no fall.

Motor comin', got no coal,
Grabbin' auger borin' hole;
Ketchum powder an' the squib,
Tamp 'em up and blow out rib.

Fetchin' buddy, put for track,
Push for place, hurt him back;
Come to place, too much smoke;
No got dog-hole—maybe choke.

Shovel fast to load-a him,
Crawl for bumper, nothin' in;
Fill him up like load of hay,
Motor come, take heem away.

Road he purty much too far,
Have to throw two time to car;
No got rail, ties and spike,
Boss he come, he make big fight.

Come outside, two car short;
Make me mad! boy I snort!
Askin' weigh boss, find my car,
He say nothin' chew cigar.

An check-weighman, he no good,
He got head-a made of wood;
Him and weigh-boss too much friends—
Next election trouble ends.

Sometime work nothin's at all,
When the big rock he done fall;
Boss he come to me and shout:
"If you no like-a take tools out."

Company cheat how much he could,
Them he say he do me good;
No good weight like before—
Take all pay for comp'ny store.[1]

That's not all—I tell-a half,
Dat's a true, no make-a laugh,
If you t'ink I tell-a lie,
Catch-a da job—make-a da try.

From United Mine Workers Journal, *April 1, 1935. Even more than other industries, mining often attracted immigrants from almost every European and Eastern European country. Few spoke English and many, as in "Pick Coal Rhythm," spoke a dialect version of it. It is difficult to track down specific meanings for the many obscure miners' terms used in the poem, but context provides enough detail to make the poem meaningful.*

---

1. Instead of paying miners in cash, coal companies often issued their own private currency, called scrip, which miners had to use to buy food and supplies (at inflated prices) from company stores.

The Fatal Gilberton Mine

Billy H. Quinn

In the dusk of early morning,
    Through a clouded and fitful glow—
Men with their lamps are tramping
    To their toil through rain and snow.

No thought intrudes to halt the feet
    In that plodding happy line,
They know not that grim death waits
    In the fatal Gilberton Mine.

With push and pull, or friendly jest;
    They are gone and the cage descends;
Gone! Deep down to earth's inside—
    Where the dark and the lamplight blends.

There to toil—to earn their way
    Below where the sun doesn't shine—
Unsuspecting, they dream of their loved ones—
    In the fatal Gilberton Mine.

Then suddenly, through the gangways,
    Comes a deafening, crashing roar!
The dreaded exploding monster
    Hurls them flat on the mine's damp floor!

There in agony—total darkness
    Bleeding and suffering in pain!
While high above them, their loved ones
    Kneel and pray in the rain.

Sad eyes gaze at the shaft-mouth—
    Filled with despairing tears—
Wives, sweethearts and little ones
    Watch as the cage appears.

Hoping that father, son or dad
    May not be there with the slain;
Praying that he may be alive
    To be happy with them again!

Then, what tragic disappointment—
    Must these heartbroken loved ones face;
When rescuers, with tear-dimmed eyes
    Bring them out from the mine of disgrace.

Their dear, loving form is now quiet—
  Who that morning stood upright and fine—
Destroyed! He's lost! To friends and home
  Because of the Gilberton Mine.

Sad hearts, in your horrible sorrow,
  Friends from the county of Schuylkill give
A heartfelt prayer for him who's gone,
  And the family dear that live.

From United Mine Workers Journal, *April 1, 1935. The poem was accompanied by the following note from the editor: "This original poem first appeared in the Pottsburgh (Pa.) Republican, January 25, 1935, and was inspired by the Gilberton mine accident which occurred January 21, 1935, and is dedicated by the author to the families of the men who lost their lives in that disaster." Thirteen miners died as a result of the accident. The Pennsylvania State Department of Mines later issued a report holding the mine owners responsible for the deaths, reporting that the "system of mining as practiced at the time of the accident made it impossible to conduct the air to all working faces, thus permitting an accumulation of gas."*

When Daddy Gets a Raise

John Hackenbury, Moshannon, Pa.

Clouds will rift,
Skies get clearer,
Paradise will seem
Much nearer,
Home itself a trifle dearer—
  When daddy gets a raise.

There'll be pictures for the wall
Pretty carpets in the hall,
Trinkets new for one and all
  When daddy gets a raise.

Day for mother
Will be brighter,
She will hug the wee ones tighter
For her tasks will be lighter—
  When daddy gets a raise.

Skies will seem
To be turning bluer,
Holes and patches will be fewer,
For the duds will all be newer,
    When daddy gets a raise.

Brother's britches need not be
Amputated at the knee,
For the baby boy of three
    When daddy gets a raise.

As the children
Swing and teeter,
I am sure they'll all look sweeter
And perhaps a little neater,
    When daddy gets a raise.

Willie's feelings
Won't be hurt,
'Cause he has to wear a shirt
Made of mother's faded skirt,
    When daddy gets a raise.

Mother's heartaches
Will be rarer,
All the world to her'll be fairer
In its joys she'll be a sharer—
    When daddy gets a raise.

From United Mine Workers Journal, *April 1, 1935.*

The Coal-Miner's Blues

Nettie M. Schoneman

Some blues are just blue
(Mine are coal-black blues),
My troubles are coming
By three's and by two's;
My Buddy he died
And I thought as I cried,
Now I'll have those coal-black blues!

If there's anything blue
It's the coal-black blues;
Coal in my hair,
Coal in my shoes;
My muscles are aching,
My back it is breaking—
And I've got the coal-black blues.

These blues are so blue
They are coal-black blues;
For my place will cave in
And my life I will lose;
My feet they are freezing,
While I go on sneezing
'Cause I've got the coal-black blues.

Blues, blues and more blues,
Are these coal-black blues—
And it comes to my mind
A new buddy I'll choose,
When the pit boss he stops
And says, "Set some more props"—
So I've got the coal-black blues.

You say they are blue
These coal-black blues?
Now I must have sharpened
These picks that I use,
I'm sick, sore and tired,
Don't care if I'm fired,
Since I've got the coal-black blues.

I'm out with these blues,
Dirty, coal-black blues.
Come drill up some holes
For the powder. Good news!
Balm for my sorrow—
We'll lay off tomorrow
Pipe down with those coal-black blues!

From United Mine Workers Journal, *March 1, 1938.*

Union Stew

Anonymous

I surely never hope to view
    A steak as luscious as a stew,
The latter is the tasty goal
    Of elements in perfect whole . . .

A mad assemblage of legumes
    Exuding warm ambrosial fumes,
Each seasoning of proper length,
    Proving in union there is strength.

A steak is gander . . . it is true,
    Yet it needs no special skill to brew.
It is an art a stew to make,
    But anyone can broil a steak.

From United Mine Workers Journal, *January 15, 1939. The poem relies on the rather ingenious conceit that the action of various ingredients coming together in a stew resembles the action of workers coming together in a union. This recipe followed the poem:*

"Two pounds beef, 1 No. 3 can tomatoes, 2 pounds potatoes (about 6 medium potatoes), 4 medium onions, 1 green pepper, 2 teaspoons salt, 1 teaspoon sugar, 1/8 teaspoon pepper, 2 teaspoons dark caramel, flour to thicken.

Cut meat in small cubes and arrange in layers with rest of ingredients except tomatoes and flour, with enough cold water to cover. Let come to a boil, add tomatoes, cover and let simmer for two hours. Mix smoothly with cold water and enough flour to thicken, add to stew and let simmer 15 minutes or longer. Sprinkle with grated cheese and serve hot.

Result—a Hungarian goulash guaranteed to put the family in a good humor. Serve it hot and give the husband a happy send off to his union meeting."

Machinery vs. Men

W. I. Williams, Shelburn, Indiana

Less than forty years ago,
The people did not think or know
That surely some day there would be
(And some of us have lived to see)
Machinery take our jobs from us
And put the country in a muss!

If we could only work and earn
Prosperity would soon return;
We'd draw our cash, we then would say:
We have some bills that we must pay;
We'll buy our families food and clothes—
That's where the workers' money goes!

We'd buy good things for us to eat,
And shoes for all our kiddies feet,
Then we'd pay for coal and rent—
When this is done our money's spent.
Now any man, though blind, can see
That work will bring pros-per-i-ty.

Machines cannot eat corn nor hay—
They have no grocery bills to pay;
They cannot talk like men, nor sing
Like birdies in the lovely Spring;
They only make a vicious hum
That puts our country on the bum!

From United Mine Workers Journal, *June 15, 1940. The poem was accompanied by the fol-
lowing note from the editor: "W. I. Williams, Shelburn, Ind., the author of these rhymes, has
passed his seventy-sixth birthday and has been a miner for over forty years and belonged to the
United Mine Workers of America ever since it started, being transferred from the old Knights
of Labor in 1886."*

The Miner

Anonymous

A miner knocked at the pearly gate,
　His face was scarred and old,
He stood before the man of fate
　For admission to the fold.

"What have you done?" St. Peter asked.
　"To gain admission here?"
"I've been a miner, sir," he said,
　"For many and many a year."

The pearly gates swung open wide
　And St. Peter touched the bell,
"Come in," he said, "And choose your harp,
　"You've had your share of hell."

From United Mine Workers Journal, *Aug. 1, 1940.*

United Packinghouse Workers of America

In the early part of the century, Upton Sinclair's novel *The Jungle* documented the dreadful living and working conditions among packinghouse workers on Chicago's South Side, conditions that two failed strikes in 1904 and 1921 did little to alter. So when the CIO announced the formation of the Packinghouse Workers Organizing Committee in 1937, it encountered a militant group of workers impatient for the chance to organize. Besides seniority, hours, and wages, packinghouse workers—like other industrial workers—objected to the sometimes brutal pace of work, what they called "the speed-up." Indeed, packinghouse workers had particular cause to object to the speed-up. Years before Henry Ford brought the assembly line to his Highland Park plant in 1914, packinghouses had used the assembly—or "disassembly"—line to move animal carcasses past fixed workers. Just as in the automobile industry, assembly line production shifted control over the pace of work from workers to foreman, who could increase or decrease the rate of production almost at will. "The Speed King," from the Packinghouse Workers newspaper, satirizes the hapless foreman who berates his workers for not working fast enough and believes he could do a better job; but it also celebrates the control over the pace of production workers partly won back when they successfully formed a union.

The Speed King

Ivan Soelberg, Local 389

I

The race horse boss was at a loss
And slowly rubbed his chin.
Beset with greed for still more speed
Ambition came to him.
Took off his frock, put up his "rock,"
A knife from pouch he took.
He got the feel of knife on steel,
Then bellowed toll he shook.

II

"Get down the line. We'll make up time.
In fact, we'll get ahead.
You think you work? You fellows shirk,
You act as if you're dead.
To do work right, stay home at night
And rest the whole night through."
He thumped his chest with zeal and zest,
"That's why I'm not like you!"

III

He seized a hide, the knife he tried,
Then sneered and pushed with might.
He beat the steel with ring peal,
His rage had reached a great height,
For snickers here and giggles there
Had stirred his twisted mind.
Each stroke he made with that big blade
Put some poor guy behind.

IV

Between the forms of butchered beasts
A flash of knife and steel,
This maniac plunging on
His methods to reveal,
To show the men how fast he was,
To let them know who's king.
He growled, he howled, then he scowled,
He followed this wild thing.

V

But the time has come to bounce this bum.
We've tamed him, held him back.
Though the wheels may hum,
Our union's come.
Yes slow-down!
We've caught the knack.

From CIO News—Packinghouse Workers Edition, *February 20, 1939.*

United Rubber Workers

Rubber workers, especially in the city of Akron, Ohio, struggled for decades to form a union and improve their working and living conditions, and throughout the second half of the 1930s, their CIO-affiliated union, the United Rubber Workers, published poetry urging on that struggle. Mary Lechner's "If This Be My Native Land" however, offers one of the most sympathetic, general indictments of life during the Great Depression in all of the published work of the 1930s. The poem appeared prominently in the second issue of *United Rubber Worker.*

If This Be My Native Land

Mary Lechner

If this be my native land, I am not proud,
For mirrored in the searching pools that plunge
And pry into the villages and towns,
Are weak and hungry faces, gaunt and streaked
With lines of rain. These are my people,
And I am bitter with their sorrow.
These are my people—and I am not proud.

Better that the willows break their tongues
Against the towering trunks and better that
The maples lose their color and gloss,
Better that the grass reject the soil

To stay in brown defeat atop the earth—
Than to have these solemn people curse their souls
And lie and look into the night with hate.

If this be my native land—I am not proud.
The darkness curls its snaky fingers round
The churning cities—it cannot conceal
The squalor of the slums, the quietness
Of hungry bodies—the odor of despair,
The groping of blind hands, the sullenness
Of eyes that lie and look into the night with hate. . .
I am not proud of this. . . my native land.

From United Rubber Worker, *November 1936.*

United Steel Workers

"Here Goes Steel!" appeared on the front page of the first issue of *Steel Labor,* the newspaper of the Steel Workers Organizing Committee (SWOC). After its split from the AFL, the CIO first attempted to organize the steel industry, and in 1937, following the sit-down strike by autoworkers in Flint, Michigan, the CIO-backed SWOC won its first and a key victory, negotiating a contract with U.S. Steel, the largest steel corporation in the country and the one most devoted to remaining "open shop," as the poem's reference to the failed, bloody Homestead, Pennsylvania, strike of 1892 suggests. James Rorty is one of the poets in this collection about whom we know some biographical information, if only because Rorty did not work in the steel mills but as an editor and as a well-known social critic of the middle decades of the twentieth century. He started out as a poet, publishing a collection, *Children of the Sun, and Other Poems,* in 1926, and went on to write influential works on public health, advertising, McCarthyism, and the labor movement; in the late 1950s and 1960s, after a shift to the political right, he produced somewhat critical articles on the civil rights movement for the journal *Commentary.*

Here Goes Steel!

James Rorty

I had a word with Pete today, and Pete sees how it stands:
It's the battle of the century, their dough against our hands.
They rooked us in the court room but we've still got our hands!

I had a word with Nick and Mike, and they're the boys can take it!
We've worn their collar long enough, and now's the time to break it.
You heard 'em yell at Homestead?[1] Well, I think we're going to make it!

They say five billion dollars can't possibly be wrong.[2]
Oh yeah? I'm betting, brother, that they sing another song
The day steel blows wide open, a million workers strong!
The tide is rising, brother, it's rising deep and cool

And Myron's[3] got his feet wet and every dick and stool
Is going to learn his lessons in a brand new school!

They've got the jitters, brother, can't you hear those fat cats squeal?
You can hear 'em in their funny papers: "There goes steel!"
There goes steel, boys; yes, there goes steel.
It's the battle of the century, for here goes steel!

From Steel Labor, *August 20, 1936.*

---

1. In 1892, the Carnegie Steel Company, under the management of Henry Clay Frick, sought to break the powerful Amalgamated Association of Iron and Steel Workers at Carnegie's enormous mill in Homestead, Pennsylvania. After Frick locked unionized workers out of the plant, the steelworkers revolted, calling a strike and, through an advisory committee, taking control over the company town itself. Frick sent three hundred Pinkerton guards from nearby Pittsburgh down the Allegheny River, but thousands of armed strikers fought back and forced the Pinkertons to surrender. In response to Frick's pleas, the governor of Pennsylvania called out the state militia, which retook the town and opened the plants. When the plants opened, Frick refused to rehire most of the striking workers, which led to the gradual decline and death of the AA and steel unionism in Homestead and across the country.
2. "Five billion" refers to the combined value of the steel companies, as in a cartoon that appeared in the following issue of *Steel Labor:* "Five Billion Dollars Worth of Steel Is Scared" when it is confronted by "The Biggest Organizing Drive in American Labor History," a brawny worker with fists raised.
3. Myron Taylor, president of U.S. Steel.

Index of Poems and Poets

Adventure, 38
All-Fighters Day, 131
Allinger, Harold, 93
Ami, Covington, 84
Amos 'n Andy, 43
Anonymous, 56, 57, 62, 65, 85, 99, 103, 110,
    156, 169, 183, 184, 211
Anonymous (From Mingo County), 203
As Uncle Henry Would Have Us Pray, 176

Barrelle, Lou, and Andy Lucas, 205
Bates, Floyd C., 195
Beefsteak Blues, 170
Begging for Bread, 49
Bishop, James M., 61
Blagden, Willie Sue, 155
Blind Justice, 160
Blue-Eyed Pigeon, 147
Brighter Ash, 56
Brocken, Albert, 100
Brother's Complaint, A, 104

Cafeteria, 149
Canadian Ford Worker, 168
Cargill, Aseneth, 56
Carter, Jessie, 130
Chaplin, Ralph, 88
Children of the Mine, 203
Coal-Miner's Blues, The, 210
Company Union, The, 102
Company Unionism, 52
Confessions, 84
Curious Christians, The, 98

Day in Technicolor, 144
Dearborn Hospitality, 177
Detroit, 180
Dignity, 141
Dillman, Martin A., 59
Discernment, 56
Don't Bite the Hand, 46
Donald, Peter, Jr., 45
Dreams 1914–1918, 158

Eight Bells, 151
England, Elizabeth, 173
Evacuations, 142

Factory Windows, 138
Fatal Gilberton Mine, The, 206
Fibres, 74
Final Installment, The, 122
Five-Point Plan, The, 193
Fordism, 184
Ford Slave, A, 168
Ford Sunday Evening Hour, 184
For Seven Years I've Roamed the Seas, 153
Forty Fathoms, 154, 158, 160, 161, 162
Fountain, Clayton, 171
Freedom, 124
Freeman, J., 153
From an Old-Timer, 69

Gequel, 52
Giovannitti, Arturo, 122, 131
Good Ol' Pete, 111
Grin, Clown, Grin, 83

Hackenbury, John, 208
Hall, Covington, 84, 97, 98, 111
Handcox, John, 112, 113, 115
Harlan, 88
*Have you ever worked on a line puttin' out five
    thousand bodies a day?,* 181
Headline Fugitive, 143
Heat Portraits, 91
Hell, 93
Help!, 194
Helper's Prayer, A, 199
Here Goes Steel!, 220
Hirschfeldt, John G., 96
Holman, E. H. H., 43
House That Jack Built, The, 173

I am the picket, 178
If This Be My Native Land, 217
I.L.G.W.U., The, 125
In a Garment Factory, 121
It's a stick-up!, 128

Jacques, Edna, 51
Just Another Day, 40

Kenney, Jack, 92
King Henry the V-8th, 167

Label Tells a Story, The, 57
Labor, 68
Labor Stage, 135
Lament of a Michigander, 195
*Landlord, What in the Heaven is the Matter
    with You?,* 113
Lechner, Mary, 217
Left Rudder, 94, 151
Lender, C., 69
Letting the Cat out of the Bag, 169
Line-Up, The, 96
Live One, The, 103
Lynch, Thomas R., 49

Machinery vs. Men, 212
Madrid, 95
Marlatt, Ralph H., 178, 180, 181, 182
McGowan, Jack, 199
McKillups, Bud, 67
Medalis, George A., 176
Men are asking for work, 36
Migratory I.W.W., The, 92
Miner, The, 213
Modestus, Mr., 36, 38, 72, 74, 76, 126, 128
Morning, 149

Mugford, Walter, 193, 194, 197
Munter, Gertrude, 34
My Picket Card, 156

Negro Seaman Speaks, The, 161
"Never Again," 197
Night Fog, 145
Ninety and Nine, The, 64
Nix, 86
Nolan, Lola, 83

On Hearing a Negro Spiritual, 130
Owen, Nell, 40

Paine, John, 167
Parent Prayer, 148
Patton, William, 86, 89
People, The, 183
Pick Coal Rhythm, 205
Planter and the Sharecropper, The, 112
Poggianni, Joseph, 203
Poll, 187
Press, Max, 125, 136
pressure, 187, 188

Questionnaire for Actors, 47
Quinn, Billy H., 206

Real Americans, 199
Reardon, Francis, 176
Revenge without Music, 46
Reverie, 46
Rimer, Al, 199
Rorty, James, 220
Roth, Murray, 172, 177
Roy, Tekla, 170

Scanlin, Francis, 47
Schoneman, Nettie M., 210
Shape Up, The, 94
Sharecropper, The, 110
Share-Cropper's Choice, 110
Shipowners' "Days," 154
Sin of Hoarding, The, 89
Skid Road, The, 85
Slogan, The, 162
Smith, Bennie, 55
Smith, Hilda W., 135
Smith, Rose Elizabeth, 64
Soelberg, Ivan, 215
Speed King, The, 215
Spring, 137

Square Deal or a "Quare" Deal, A, 61
Steltemeier, R. F., 102
Stevenson, Martha, 124
Stick, Boys!, 55
Stitching Machine, 140
Stoolie's Lament, A, 172
Supreme Court, 62
Surpluses, O the Surpluses!, 97
Surplus Value, 65

Tane, Miriam, 137, 138, 140, 141, 142, 143, 144, 145, 147, 148, 149
T-Bone Slim, 87
310 Bulletin, 91
Thursday Afternoons, 176
To a Nine-Inch Gun, 99
To Alfred P. Sloan, 171
To the Seamen of the International Brigades, 155
To the Spinachers, 100
To Whom It May Concern . . . , 136
Tobie, 184
Thursday Afternoons, 176
"Trust in the Profit System!," 76
Turning the Corner (The Romantic Quest of Lost Love), 87

Union Stew, 211
Union Song, The, 115

Verses from West Virginia, 203

Waitresses' Union No. 249, 59
Waller, Syde, 134
We are the auto workers, 182
We talk of progress, 126
West, Thomas H., 65
What Do You Build?, 134
What We Want, 172
When Daddy Gets a Raise, 208
While Playing Santa Claus, 65
Whitaker, Robert, 95
Why, oh why?, 72
Williams, W. I., 212
Willoughby, Lee, 46
Winthrop, Ann, 46
Wizard of Robot, The, 34
Working Mother's Prayer, 51

Yood, Nahum, 121
Young, George F., 172
"you work tomorrow," 188